A Woodcarver's Workbook # 2

More Great Carving Projects

by Mary Duke Guldan

Box 7948
Lancaster, PA 17604

© 1994 by Fox Chapel Publishing

Publisher:	Alan Giagnocavo
Project Editor:	Ayleen Stellhorn
Cover Design:	Dennis Shirk
Photography:	Bob Arnold Studios

Manufactured in the United States of America

ISBN #1-56523-037-X

To order your copy of this book,
please send check or money order for cover price plus $2.00 to:
Fox Chapel Book Orders
Box 7948
Lancaster, PA 17604-7948

Try your favorite book supplier first!

Table of Contents

Dedicated to Aunt Pat and the Beanfield Buddies, who have a lot of ideas...

FORWARD!

wayward?

untoward.

Before we get down to serious beavering~

Always wear eye protection!

Save your eyes from flying objects

Where are they getting these ideas?

out in the backyard, I reckon.

Nose protection too, where there's dust!

Long shanked blades (like gouges and chisels) are 2-handed tools!
BOTH HANDS BEHIND THE BLADE!

Is it all downhill from here?

(Push; don't pull!) As with other user-unfriendly tools, never aim at anything (yourself especially!) that you don't want to hit.

We've taken some liberties with the poses to make figures sturdy and not so likely to tip over so easily. They're designed to keep you from having carving and engineering problems.

(whenever possible)

Let's take a little tour of the tool box...

First we'll chase the wild life out.

Use the equipment which suits you best. These items are for reference, as they are mentioned as they contribute to these projects.

You'll need a saw, but since your blank is made out of layers of lumber, you won't need access to a bandsaw. A coping saw, scroll saw or jigsaw will do splendidly.

We give quite a workout to two popular power tools, the Foredom grinder and AutoMach (reciprocal) carver. These tools liberate one from having to secure the project to a bench or stand, an essential and problematic aspect of carving with a mallet and gouges and chisels. The power tools have a variety of changeable cutters, so can be used on a project from start to finish.

The Foredom grinder spins various burrs, cutters and abrasives in a small handpiece at the end of a flexible shaft. Its speed is regulated by pressure on a foot pedal.

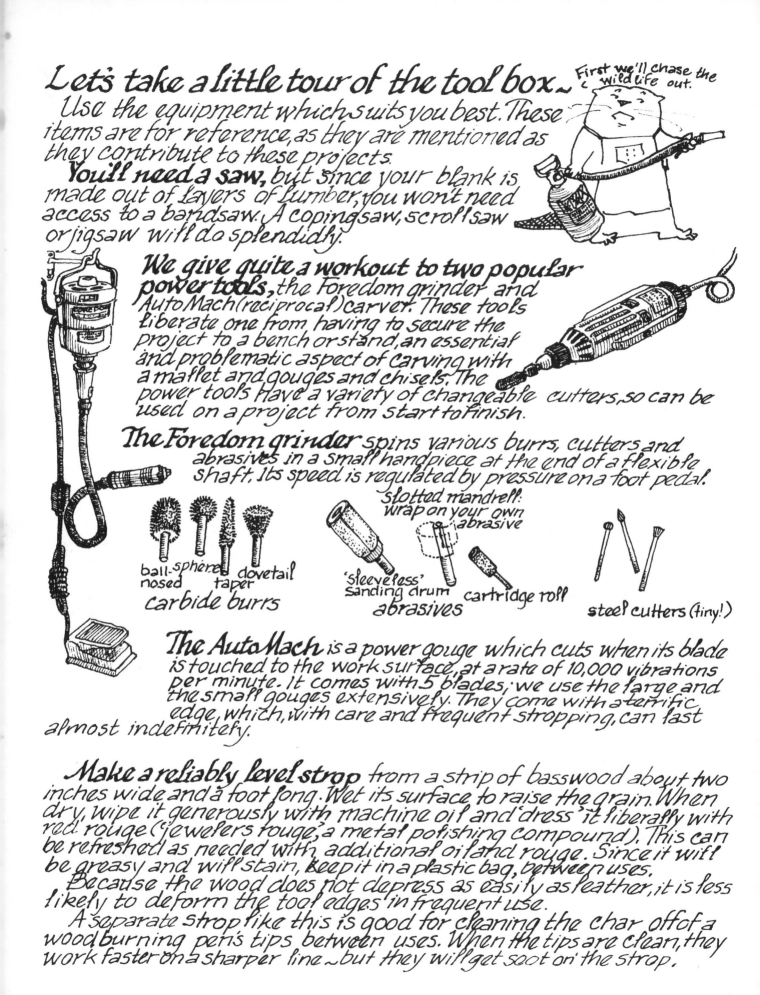

ball-nosed · sphere · taper · dovetail

carbide burrs

slotted mandrel: wrap on your own abrasive

'sleeveless' sanding drum **abrasives**

cartridge roll

steel cutters (tiny!)

The AutoMach is a power gouge which cuts when its blade is touched to the work surface, at a rate of 10,000 vibrations per minute. It comes with 5 blades; we use the large and the small gouges extensively. They come with a terrific edge, which, with care and frequent stropping, can last almost indefinitely.

Make a reliably level strop from a strip of basswood about two inches wide and a foot long. Wet its surface to raise the grain. When dry, wipe it generously with machine oil and 'dress' it liberally with red rouge ('jewelers rouge,' a metal polishing compound). This can be refreshed as needed with additional oil and rouge. Since it will be greasy and will stain, keep it in a plastic bag, between uses.

Because the wood does not depress as easily as leather, it is less likely to deform the tool edges in frequent use.

A separate strop like this is good for cleaning the char off of a wood burning pen's tips between uses. When the tips are clean, they work faster on a sharper line – but they will get soot on the strop.

A woodburner can be a very valuable asset, added to your kit. 'Pyrographic pens' (now that they've got custom tips and dial-set variable heat settings) are not just for fur and feather detailing.

Remember how the Homeric hero, Odysseus, hardened the end of a spar in a fire to use as a spear to battle the Cyclops, a monsterous giant... and pioneers scorched the bottoms of fence posts in pits of hot coals to harden them and to retard rot before they were used... We make that time-honored technology work for us. On figures to be painted or stained so the char won't show, use that 'pen' to stopcut and stabilize fragile outlines of nostrils, lips, ear openings~clefts between cleats on cloven hooves~paws and claws~ shoes and soles on horses' hooves~ strapwork on harness...

Pens with 'replaceable tips' have an interchangeable variety of points which plug into the hand piece.

This will cut as well as draw

This can poke in confined areas. Use your knife point to trim a tiny sliver at right angles to your burned line to raise the strap from the animal's hide...

Gouges texture surfaces beautifully, as well as carving the bone and muscle masses that give the shape and character to a figure. Standard 'basic tool' sets include a mixture of gouges, chisels and a veiner~ready to use. There usually are two gouges, fine for us; one wider and shallow, the other deep and narrow.

A valuable addition is a ½ inch wide shallow fishtail gouge, named for the flaring edges of its blade. It is an excellent surfacing tool because its cuts are broad, open and not deep. It suggests muscles and the lay of hair/fur. The flared blade can reach into confined areas.

Micro carving tools, sets of ultra-miniaturized chisels, gouges and veiners are excellent for detailing. They were developed for ship modelers however~sculptors tend to break them quite easily. Take it easy~they are fun to use!

Detailing knives stopcut, surface, trim, shape and level areas for additions (like applying the arm to the shoulder location. A sabre-clip blade like a nonfolding pocket knife does all kinds of scribing and trimming. It can also be used for handsome surfacing, leaving sketchy, shallow cuts.

A stiff, straight-edged blade is the most reliable and maneuverable for stopcuts. It is required to level the matching areas where arms and shoulders meet.

Now, let's put those tools to work!

Three Bears

BECAUSE their bodies and legs are sturdy and less intricate than those of our other undertakings, we'll use the bears as "student" pieces, working through each step of the project in considerable detail. Read over reference notes about the bear and consider the options carefully before you begin planning your piece.

Biologists explain that the grizzly and the Alaskan brown bear are so similar in body shape and color that their most easily distinguishable differences are size (brownies are bigger) and claw length (grizzlies' are longer). In view of the incredible strength and bulk of these splendid mammals, such considerations are about equal to the concept that poisonous snakes can be recognized by the elliptical pupils of their eyes. When surprised by a live, loose specimen, no one I know is going to pause long enough to look at such small distinguishing details.

The bear's environment will determine your particulars; grizzlies and elk share the same range, as do brownies and salmon. Therefore, the grizzly with the dead elk will be posed by some suggestion of water, as he would probably not have tackled a healthy elk. Since elk will readily cross water and do drown, your opportunistic grizzly must have come upon this carcass when the rain-swollen river receded. Since local coyotes have well-worn paths down in the river bottom where they scavenge the occasional deer and cattle carcasses, wolves certainly do the same.

Your carving will tell a little story, then, so think out the scenario before you start to carve. One good idea leads to another—so let's go!

To use these patterns...
(First you sort out that tangle of legs!)

Most patterns have alternate poses, in addition to the main one drawn in a solid line, with the other side of the body indicated in dots; the trunk is dot-and-dash. The other pose options are shown in a broken line. Take your pick!

Trace and cut out your pattern choice, marking the legs or side of the body nearest you.

1. Check the diagram showing layers for lamination. Trace only the parts of each layer that you will actually need. Lamination reduces waste.

By 'building' your blank out of more readily available lumber, you can dodge flaws. Scraps will be used for small additions and accessories. Lumber can be cut with a small saw.

If your lumber is not wide enough for your pattern, 'piece' together layers. Divide the pattern through the trunk with a series of staggered joints. Crease the pattern over the edge of the lumber to show the division exactly. Be sure to identify the sections of each layer. Watch grain direction!

2. When all of the pieces have been cut out, spread glue on Layer 1 and stack Layer 2 on top, 'tacking' thin nails through it to keep the layers aligned. Carefully apply a couple of clamps to sturdy areas of the body. (Very small screw-type clamps on the extremities, like head and legs, insure good glue contact.)

Let the glue 'set' (get thick and sticky: yellow carpenters' glue will do this in an hour or two.)

When the glue has 'set', carefully (so as not to disturb the glue bond), remove clamps and 'tacks.' (Small, slender nails, used by apiarists to build frames for beehives, called 'wire' nails in hardware stores. make great 'tacks.' Fence pliers drive (1.), pull (2.) and straighten (3.) them.)

protect your wood; use a scrap of leather belt

Assembling the blank~

If your layers are going to be 'pieced', this can be done during construction of the blank~ put down a piece of thin plastic, (an old shopping bag) to keep from sticking your project to your workbench.

Spread glue on the edges of the pieces to abut each other, forming the layer. Align them carefully. Apply glue on top and stack on the next layer, edge-gluing its pieces as needed. Pinch-dogs, ⊔ staple type clamps, are not required on such small scale. Check alignment, then 'tack' in a couple of locations per piece.

If your workbench top is level and will allow, you might clamp your piece right to it. You can put one of your clamps right on the glue seam to keep it from buckling~ it's a little messy, but works.

Let your pieced blank get nearly dry before you remove the clamps and 'tacks.'

3. Go on to complete the blank, gluing and stacking one layer at a time, 'tacking' and clamping as before. Let the glue 'set' between each layer before removing the clamps and 'tacks,' in order to add the next layer.

When the blank is complete, let it dry thoroughly, over~ night, before removing the clamps and tacks.

Figuring out where to carve~

4. Plan with your pencil, ahead of your blade! Checking front, back and dorsal views as needed, draw the outline of your project on the top (and bottom...), front and back of your blank. Don't worry with features or details; you need outside dimensions: what's waste and what's not. A centerline, approximating the backbone and center of the skull, is helpful.

Locate paws (hooves or feet...) on the 'soles' of the blank by drawing 'footprint' sized ovals. Draw an oval of muzzle size on the front of the blank.

"Gentlemen, start your engines!"

5. Let's carve! With your largest ball-nosed carbide burr in your Foredom grinder, or largest gouge in your Automach carver begin roughing out on the rump of your project. Begin at the highest peak of the hip and knock off corners toward the tail until the rump gets rounded. Repeat this procedure on the corresponding area on the other side. Compare them continually; watch for balance and symetry.

Next, hew along the top of the back, forming a slight peak; it becomes fuller over the shoulder. In most quadrupeds, the top of the ribcage, as it joins the backbone, is narrower than the bottom where the ribs are more rounded. In most four-leggers, the ribs are oval at the shoulder end; round back by the hips. The shoulders broaden above the forearms, and we take on the head and neck. Starting at the widest part of both, cutting the larger curve over the top of the skull, tapering the muzzle. Features get material left for them, but no detailing.

6. From the head, let's go to the feet. If you've had success in the roughing out using your larger tools, and the piece is not too fragile, continue with the big burr or blade. Otherwise, change to a smaller sphere burr or small gouge.

Starting on the hind feet, turning the blank over so that you can see the 'footprint' oval on the soles, trim around each outline to establish the location of each foot. From there, work your way up the outside, then the inside of each leg. Leave them quite square at first, until you match the front and back profile line in pencil.

That having been done, you will then need to round out the front and taper the back of each leg.

Your project is looking pretty recognizable already!

Surfacing~

7.
Automach users have a nearly finished surface as is, needing to have stray splinters and distracting bumps or shadows removed and the hair direction refined.

Foredom users have some interesting options. Their burred surface can be smoothly stylized down to a satin finish with abrasives, or it can be textured with gouges, a knife or a 'burning pen.'

In either event, your tool strokes need to follow the direction and texture of the fur and/or the shape of the body underneath.

For a stylized interpretation, your sculpting will be done by sanding to refine the shapes. By using progressively finer grit abrasives, (the bigger the number on the sandpaper, the smaller its scratchy particles...) you can get quite a silky surface~ lovely in an oil finish or stain, later on.

Texturing can be a lot of fun! There are several degrees of involvement: 1. gouge or knife broad-planed cuts~ perhaps followed by 2. carved or 3. woodburned fur detail. Whichever you choose, they all begin with blade work.

First, a Fuss: Keep both hands behind that gouge blade!

Thou shalt not maim nor mutilate thyself!

Cradle your project on a padded bench hook. This ingenious tray holds a linoleum block (used in block printing) hooked to the edge of a table for carving. You can custom make one of sturdy ¾ inch plywood, adding an extra bar (glued and screwed securely) to form a corner. Treat yourself to an old terrycloth bath towel at a garage sale; fold and roll it to pad your carving.

(Yes, the towel gets a few dings, but you don't.) Power the gouge with one hand (usually your right); guide with the fingers of the other hand, whose heel is braced on the project, steadying it against the padded back of the bench hook.

We mean to keep you intact, at least until the next project.

That same 'two-fisted' approach can give you excellent control over your knife. While your dominant hand supplies the power, the thumb of your other hand adds finesse by pushing on the blade's back, down near the tip. The heel of that hand braces the project against the back rail of the bench hook.

Don't worry with detailing yet, just get that body in good shape! The best texture strokes are many little shallow scoops of a curve-edged blade, such as a shallow ½ inch wide fishtail gouge, or a sabre clip (curved at the tip) knife. Cuts are irregular, don't form a distracting pattern, or cause strong shadows.

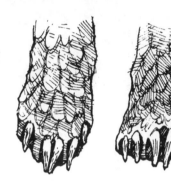

Tails and details~

8. To prevent breakage, finish your detailing in reverse order of frailty; least fragile features first, like face and paws or hooves, followed by the most breakable bits~ ears, tail and antlers last.

Since the bears have only negligible tails and no antlers, but do have splendid fur, let's go!

First, take your pencil, check your diagrams and draw in the features. Draw a line down the center of the bear's face, crossing it at eye level, to help locate the eyes, getting them as evenly spaced as possible, low and small, near the bridge of the nose. The center line can become the cleft down the front of nose and upper lip. The nostrils are large and close together. The lips show in front, mostly are underneath the muzzle. Mark the ears, checking from head on to insure that they are even.

Count toes carefully as you draw them; most paws have four each, with dewclaws on the forefeet. Bears have five each, fore and aft.

9. Use a small gouge to impress stop cuts around each eye. Rock the tool to cut into the corners for greater depth. Use the tip of your detailing knife to round the eyeballs.

If this figure is to be stained or painted so the char won't show, using the 'burning' pen instead of the knife to stopcut the mouth and claws forestalls the wood's tendency to crumble. Shaving away a sliver alongside the burn-cut raises the lips and claws. This technique also defines the pads of the raised paws.

Undercut the clawtips only if your wood has not proven to be too soft and the figure will be mounted firmly on a sturdy base.

Since the insides of the bear's ears are protected from insect invasion by profuse wooly hairs, only a few shallow scoops from a small gouge are needed to hollow the ears the least bit. Use that little gouge also to refine the cupped shapes of the backs of the ears.

Ream out the bear's nostrils with a tiny sphere cutter.

Now, for the Fur~

This has a tendency to get pretty hairy.

major's meltdown!

10. First, this bear does not need to be completely furred all in the same day! Second~ no, this hair-raising experience need not take the rest of your natural life! 'Fur' a little; take a break...

Now, let's apply our efforts to the bear.

The surface has already been lightly textured with knife or gouge cuts, which give it interesting light-catching facets. It can be left this way. Or you can expand your repertoire.

If you used a handsomely grained or colored wood, you won't want to waste its natural beauty by burning. So, you carve hair, using successively smaller tools and cuts.

You started with gouge cuts; let's take a closer look and a smaller gouge, and nip out little chips scattered through the previous cuts to make the coat more rugged.

Last pass is with your detail knife, slivering out narrow chips to form strong, shadowed, matted hair clumps in little clusters Wow, that's good looking!

If you'd rather 'burn', check the hair direction diagram back in the 'surfacing' section; pencil some of those arrows on your figure...and make some fur fly!

A rounded tip kept stropped clean and sharp really does the trick

Short-haired areas get tiny strokes from the tip of the nearly vertical tool(slightly askew)

Most hair will be five strokes clustered, fanned out, overlapping. With a couple of deep strokes, dig out a chip every so often. Handsome!

What if the first bear covets this bear's fishing spot...

This will not be a welcome intrusion.

Layer 4

Layer 3

Layer 2

Layer 1
Grain

Layers for lamination: cut and carve the fish separately

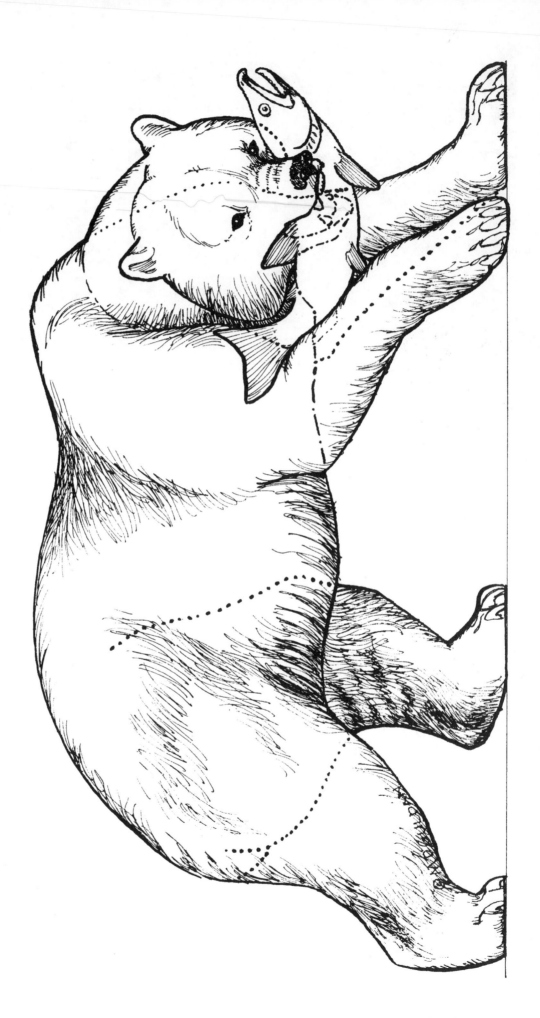

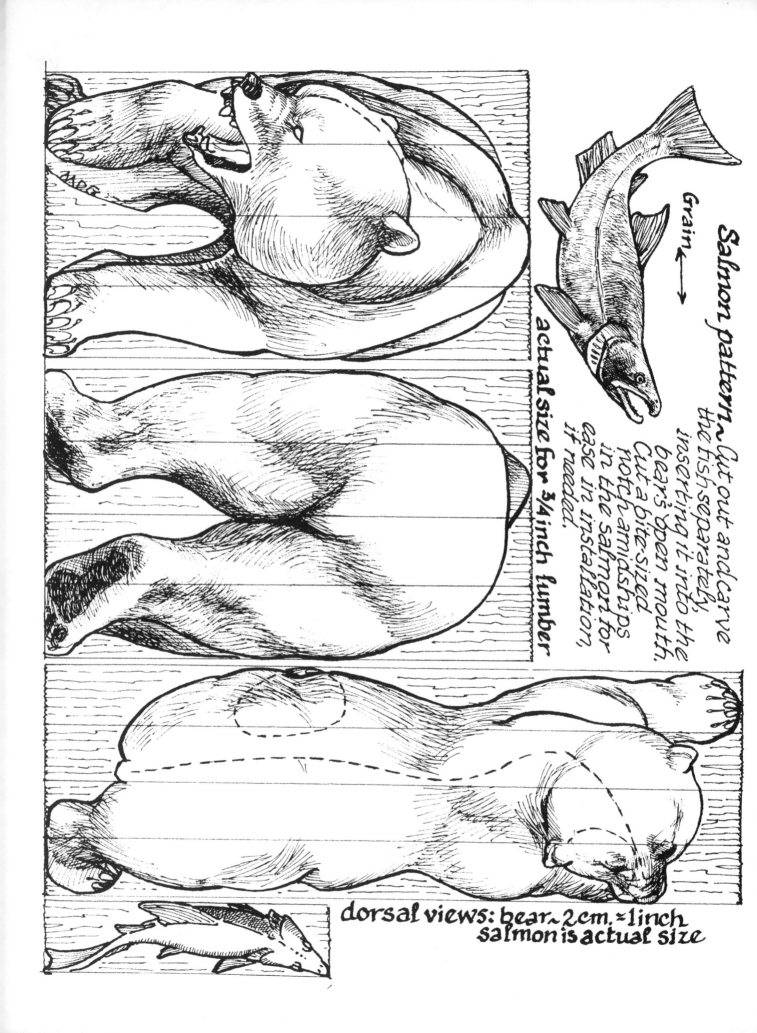

Salmon pattern~ Cut out and carve the fish separately, inserting it into the bear's open mouth. Cut a bite-sized notch amidships in the salmon for ease in installation, if needed.

Grain →

actual size for ~3/4 inch lumber

dorsal views: bear~ 2 cm. ≈1 inch
salmon is actual size

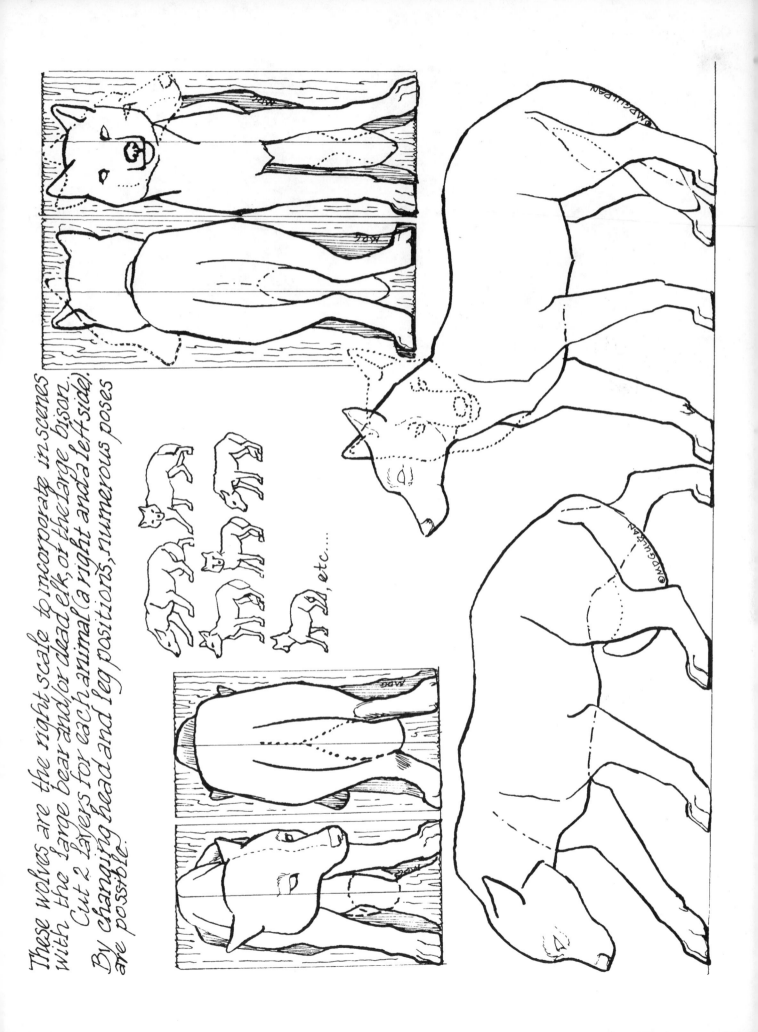

These wolves are the right scale to incorporate in scenes with the large bear and/or dead elk, or the large bison.
Cut 2 layers for each animal (a right and a left side).
By changing head and leg positions, numerous poses are possible.

etc....

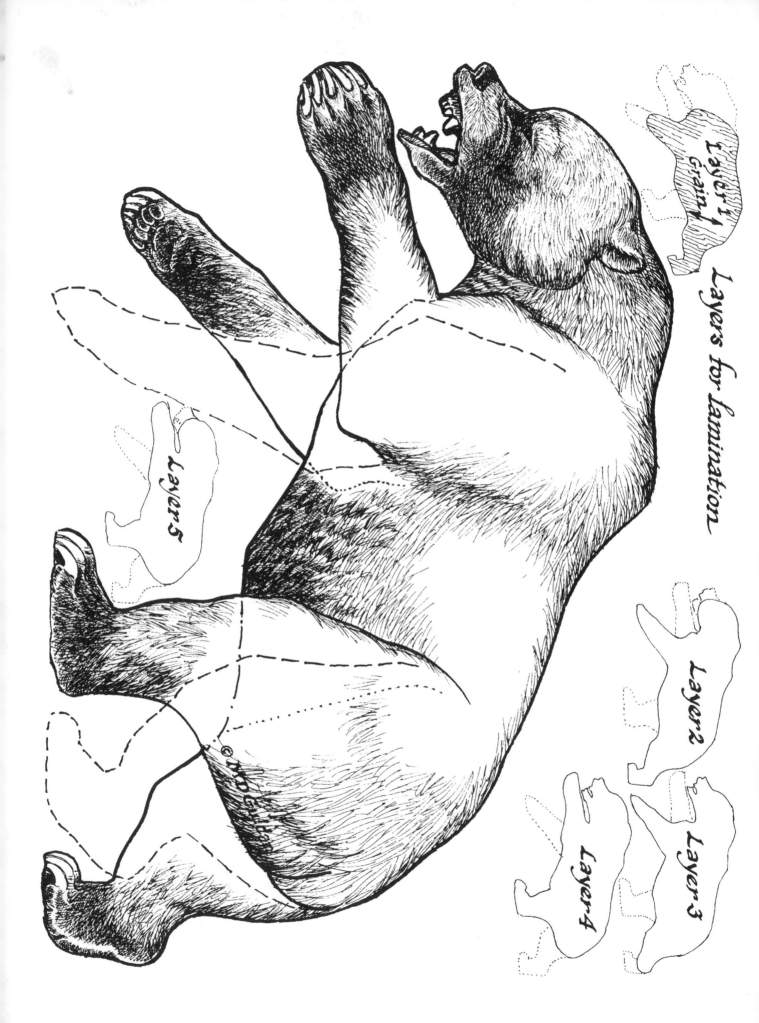

Layer 1 Grain↑

Layers for Lamination

Layer 5

Layer 2

Layer 3

Layer 4

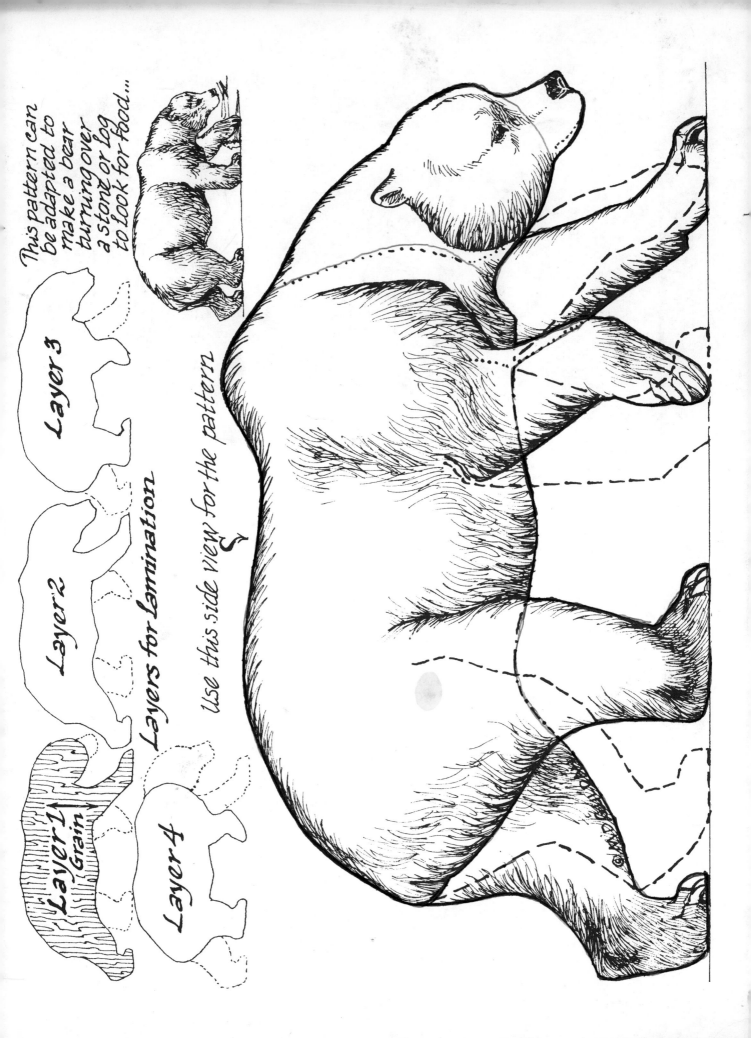

This pattern can be adapted to make a bear turning over a stone or log to look for food...

Layer 3

Layer 2

Layers for lamination

Layer 1
Grain

Layer 4

Use this side view for the pattern

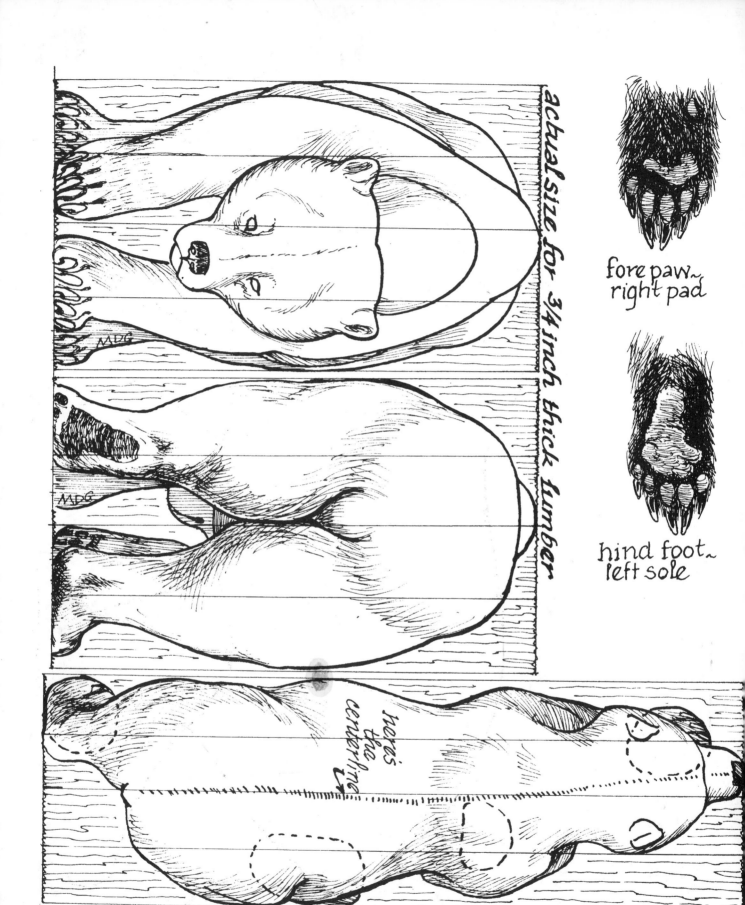

actual size for 3/4 inch thick lumber

MDG

MDG

fore paw~
right pad

hind foot~
left sole

here's
the
centerline ↙

dorsal view: 2 cm. = 1 inch ~ with 'foot print' ovals to help you
position the bear's paws on the
bottom of the blank...

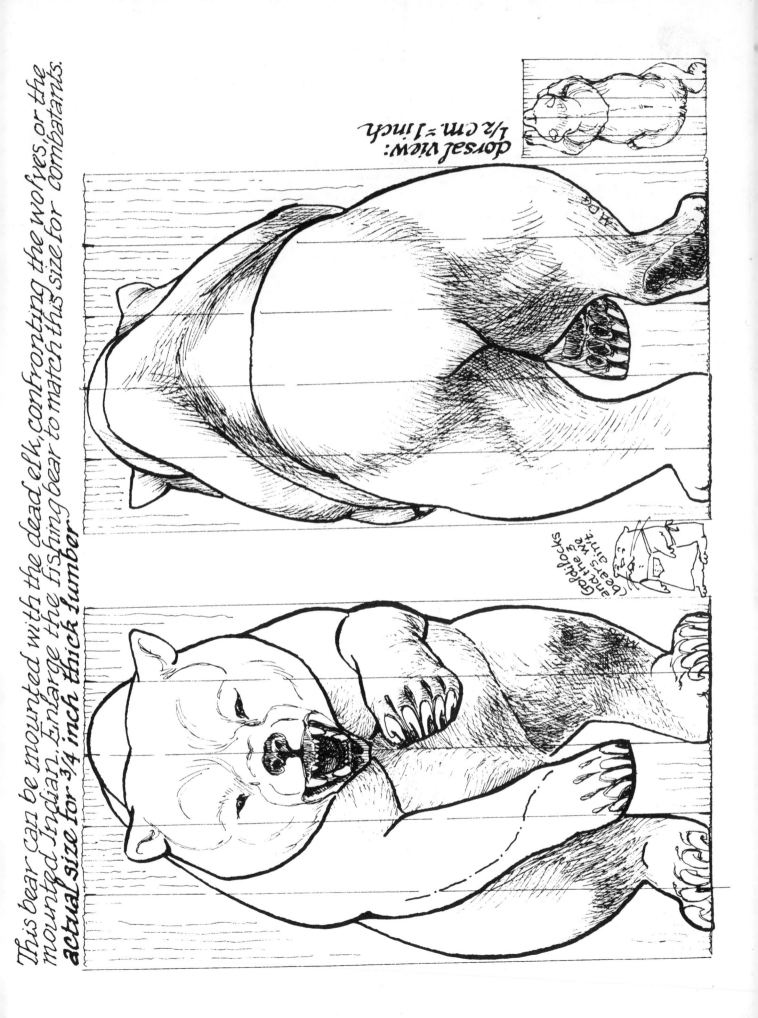

This bear can be mounted with the dead elk, confronting the wolves, or the mounted Indian. Enlarge the fishing bear to match this size for combatants. **actual size for 3/4 inch thick lumber**

dorsal view: 1/2 cm = 1 inch.

MPG

Goldilocks and the 3 bears shirt.

Bison

IF you are inexperienced in carving hoofed quadrupeds, have no fear. The bison, with his forelegs shrouded in coarse hair, is only half as fragile as other four-legged grazers. Rather than the basic buffalo, you may opt for the more dynamic pivoting pose. An alternate pose incorporates wolves surrounding a bull. These predators would not reasonably tackle a healthy bull; however, biologists have photographed wolves interacting with moose at a national park on Isle Royale in northwest Lake Superior. The wolves will often harass moose that they obviously have no intention of killing, as if testing the moose's mettle. One might infer that wolves will do the same to bison. You may also decide to pose the bison with your Indian figure. Albino bison did occur occasionally; the Indians viewed them as special omens. If you decide not to reposition your mounted Indian to fire a quick arrow, he can be regarding this bison as a sacred albino. To show a bison sparring with another bull, straighten the leading foreleg and trace a repeat of the thrusting, farthest hind leg.

You will notice that because of his vertical, slab-sided physique, the bison needs only four laminated layers. By this time, you are probably proficient in laminating and have the previous projects for reference, so let's concentrate instead on anatomy. The technique will be the same, with basic shaping starting from back to front, up the animal's back, using your largest ball-nosed burr or AutoMach gouge.

1. The tailhead ridge is shorter in the bison, and the slope from buttocks to hip is much steeper than the bull's. Whereas the bull's backline was relatively level, the bison's is narrow and inclined up toward the hump. The bull's barrel is quite rounded, top and bottom, but the lumbar vertebrae (see Cross Section E) form a pronounced shelf, which is obscured in the bull by marbled fat/muscle tissue, but quite obvious in the bison.

As you work toward the back of the bison's shoulders, refer to Cross Section D, then C and the starred area in Figure 1. Form a slight hollow behind the shoulder blade, below the shaggier hair growing along the upper ridge of the hump.

The dense, woolly hair is even shaggier on the forward top side of the hump and ridge of the neck, softening the wedge-shaped character of the hump. The hair is extremely thick, becoming creased from bending. Check Cross Sections B, A, D, and Figure 1 for the fullness across the top and the concave area just below.

2. At this point, having worked from one side to the other all the way up the animal's back, hump, and neck, you will be ready to rough-in his head.

The pattern was planned for a sparring bison pair, so the dense crown is somewhat crushed. If your bison will be a single figure, you may want to add the extra fullness, most pronounced in older bulls, by referring to the profile in Figure 1.

The head is best begun at the muzzle, working sides first, then top and bottom. Use the muzzle detail for a face-first view. The bison's muzzle is a typical squared and flattened

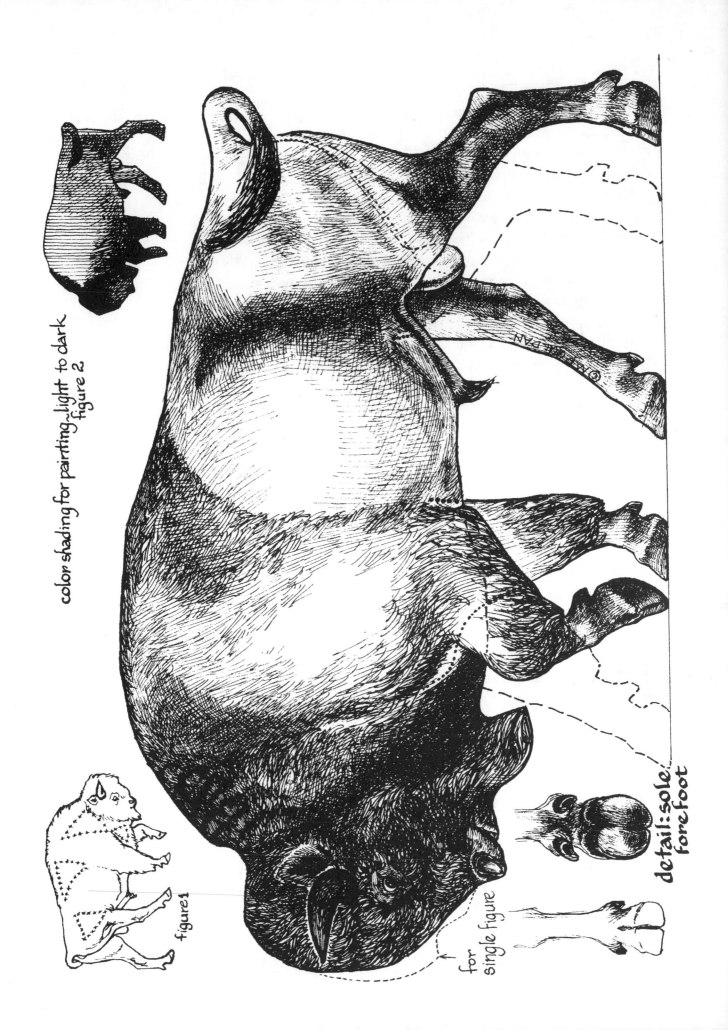

color shading for painting~light to dark
figure 2

figure 1

for single figure

detail: sole:
fore foot

bovine muzzle. The detail shows relaxed nostrils for a single figure. The pattern shows a bison with nostrils distended from the exertion of fighting.

From the head-on view, you will notice that the mounds of woolly hair obscure the facial bone structure, though the hair immediately around the eyes is very short. There is an obvious cushion over the bridge of the nose and an immense and imposing crown of longer hair over the top of the head nearly filling the space between the horns. Remember to leave enough of a projection to accommodate ears as well as horns.

3. The forelegs, with their coarse fringes of hair, will be less fragile than hind legs, so you may want to do them first. Because the bison has such a short underline, it will be to your advantage to have some of the leg "waste" out of your way.

A small gouge or carbide taper burr may be your best bet in the cramped area between the forelegs and the dewlap behind the beard. Use the tool to shape the forelegs, starting from hoof to shoulder where practical. Note that bison forefeet are rounded and have the narrowest of spaces between the hoof cleats. The dewclaws are most pronounced, projecting at almost a right angle from the leg, rather than downward as in the bull.

The bony portions of the bison's legs, both fore and hind, are very slender when seen from the front, being quite flattened on the sides. The fur comes to a point behind the legs.

4. When you reach the rib cage, you may want to switch to the large BN burr or gouge, keeping an eye on Cross Sections C and D. While there is not so appreciable a bulge of muscle above and behind the forearm because of the heavy hair, the bottom of the barrel is quite rounded, with a concave area right before the sheath.

The sheath itself is a raised ridge, as in Cross Section E, with the swell of the barrel rounding out above it on either side.

5. While in actual practice bison leave a path a scant 12 inches wide when walking single file, feet that are as closely paced in the carving as they are in life would make the carving difficult to balance. To make the bison's sparring convincing, those feet are to be firmly braced and more widely separated.

Observe that from the back view, the bison is spare and angular; his flanks are flatter. In Figure 1, you'll note a slight triangular hollow caused by the muscles stretched between the front and back points of the pelvic bones and the "knee" where the hind leg joins the body. The hind legs are very noticeably flattened at the sides; the hock joints are narrow, as seen from front or back. Note the spreading dewclaws.

While you have a large burr or gouge in hand, you may want to generalize the tail shape. This bison's tail is switching angrily.

6. Now, switch to a smaller blade or taper burr to begin the detailing in smaller spaces. Start with the head first, cleaning up around the nostrils and muzzle, defining the ridges formed by hair masses behind the jaw and beard, over eyes, and under cheeks, and clearing horns and ears from crown hair.

Sharpen up the dewclaws on all four legs, emphasizing the cleft between them in the

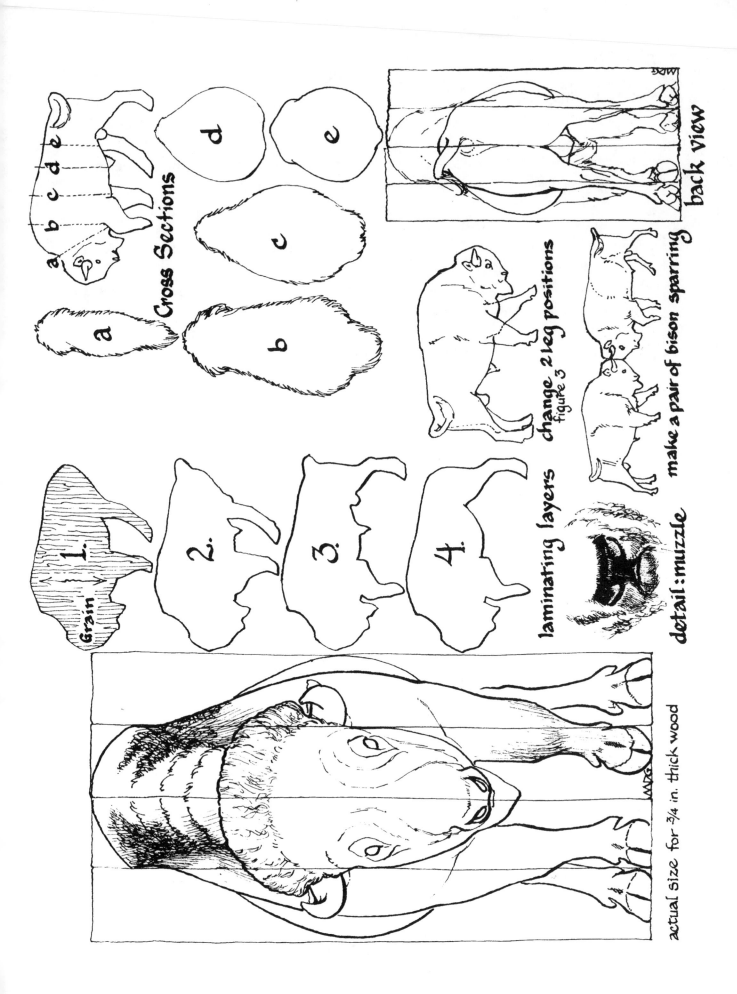

Cross Sections

a b c d e

d

e

c

a

b

change 2 leg positions
figure 3

make a pair of bison sparring

back view

laminating layers

detail: muzzle

1. Grain

2.

3.

4.

actual size for 3/4 in. thick wood

Bison

back; narrow the "ankles" immediately below them. While the point of shoulder and the hollow behind the elbow don't amount to much because of the hair, both these areas need to cast slight shadows.

A carving drill may prove most manageable, used obliquely in a shaving fashion, to refine horns and ears, tail and scrotum, hoof cleats and dewclaws.

A small steel burr does nostrils and the insides of the ears most easily.

7. To finish, you may wish to sand the hindquarters to show the shortness and thinness of the hair (to the point of near nakedness on the belly), in contrast to the improbable woolliness of the forequarters.

The hair is longest and thickest on the extremes—along the face, crown, neck and top of hump, and on the beard and legs. Here you can have a texturing "field day," because you are not committed to a whole animal. As with the bear's surface, your knife or gouge can make a rugged surface suggesting the density of the woolly hair with many little shallow scooping cuts, followed up by more texturing done with little nips of a smaller gouge. The bison's surface gets small incised slivers cut with the tip of your detailing knife, especially all along the edges of the thick fur and in the creases where the fur mats from motion, like the top of the neck, the backs of the knees, and the beard.

Instead of using all knife-work, you may want to follow your gouge strokes that first cleaned and defined this furry area with texture burned in to simulate the lay of the hair. Use lighter, shorter, shallower strokes where the hair is shorter, like on the sides and edges where hump and barrel merge. Deeper, darker strokes will show the longer hair.

In either approach, the coarse hairs of the tail and the tassel at the end of the sheath are rather sparse, so keep your texturing cuts or strokes sparse as well.

Should you decide to paint, Figure 2 will help you locate your tonal areas, from the sandy cinnamon color (burnt sienna, diluted) at the topsides of the hump, through the addition of burnt umber to get the warm dark brown that seems the main body color, to a mixture of raw umber and a tiny bit of black for the darkest areas. The color varies from one individual to another, along with their degree of "sunburn." Horns, hooves, and the nose and lips are shiny black.

When the bison's attention is tightly focused forward, his ear and eye muscles are, as with most other grazers, somehow coordinated. When his ears strain forward, projecting at right angles to his head to determine what danger lurks, his eyes roll forward in their sockets to focus forward as well. The sclera (or "white" of the eye) shows; it has a muddy, brownish tint, rather than bone white. His eyes are such a dark brown that they look black. When the paint has dried, add a tiny dot of white to highlight the eyes and the nose.

Pose a single bison at the edge of a wallow, a bowl-shaped depression in bare dirt made by buffalo gouging with hooves and horns to loosen the soil in which they can roll. A fighting pair is best posed on a rugged gouge-textured surface, suggesting trampled prairie grasses... and your imagination has taken off, conjuring up other scenes.

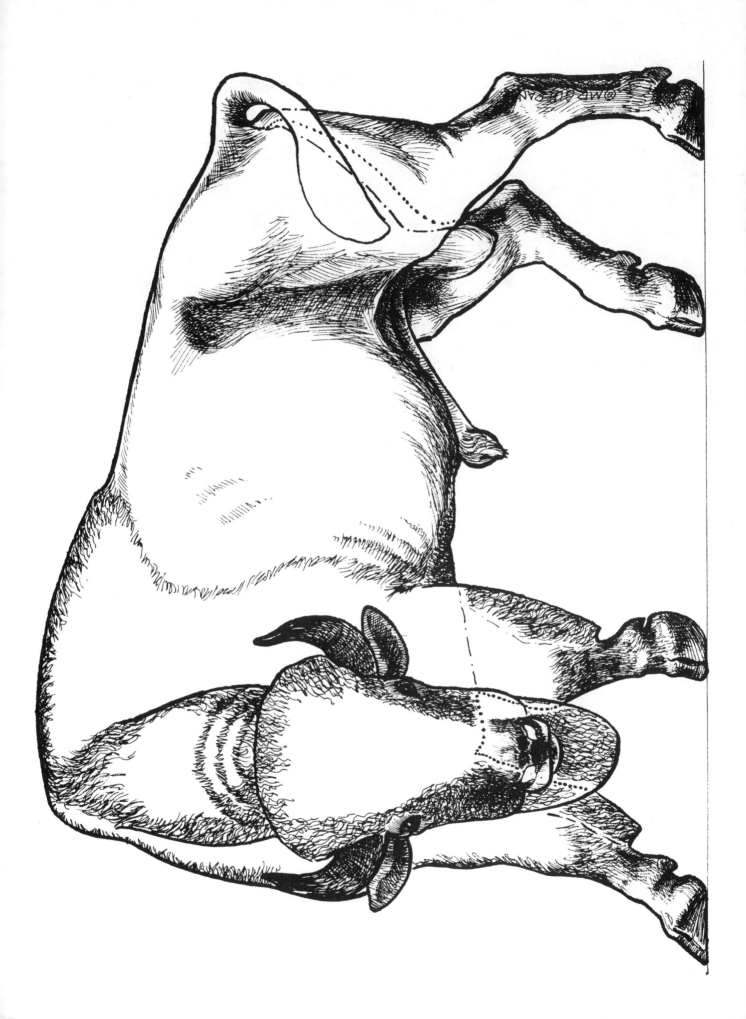

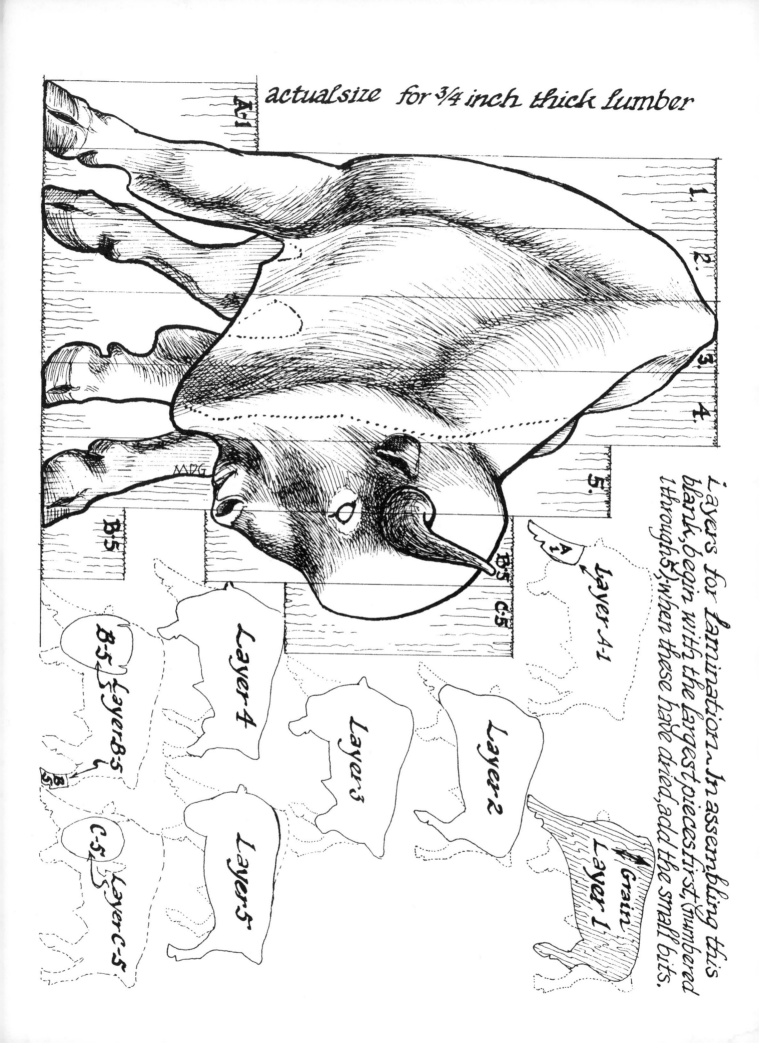

actualsize for ¾ inch thick Lumber

Layers for lamination: In assembling this blank, begin with the largest pieces first (numbered 1 through 5); when these have dried, add the small bits.

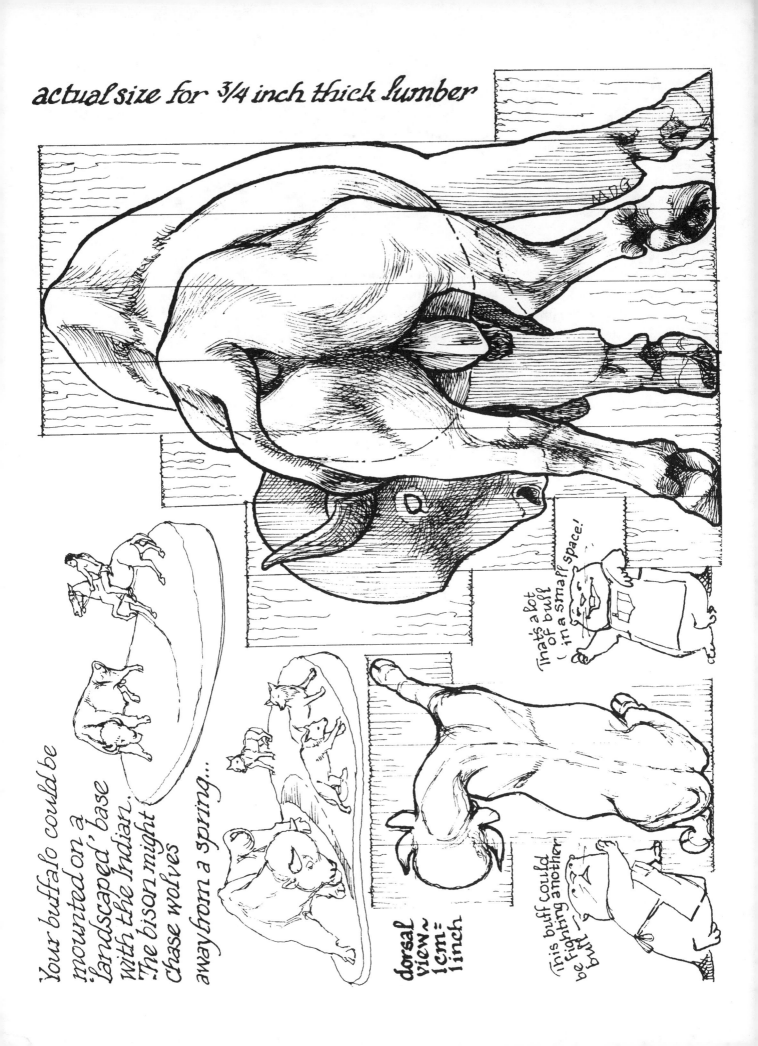

actual size for 3/4 inch thick lumber

Your buffalo could be mounted on a "landscaped" base with the Indian. The bison might chase wolves away from a spring...

dorsal view ~ 1cm = 1 inch

That's a lot of buff in a small space!

This buff could be fighting another buff —

Mules, Driving and Draft Horses

MULES have been enjoying quite a resurgence in popularity, making them a versatile subject for carving. The sterile hybrid offspring of a horse and donkey, the mule combines the horse's size with the donkey's strength, endurance, and thrifty pragmatism.

Mules were the preferred means of transport during the Renaissance, when their surefootedness was especially appreciated on roads that were often little more than cow paths. Spanish jennets, small, cream-colored saddle mules bred to amble, were coveted as the Cadillac of their day because their brisk running-walk was so easy on their riders.

Ever the farmer at heart, George Washington was delighted to received two "mammoth" jacks from the King of Spain. "Royal Gift" seems to have been the progenitor of the first mules in America. These marvels fascinated farmers for miles!

It's hard to picture our old mule with such a noble heritage, especially if you met her down in the bend of the road on your way to school. By that time she had already been quite busy, having opened a gate to let herself and all the cows out to mill in the road, or having bounced over a fence to lead half the dogs, and a good many of the neighbors, on a cross-country scamper through the fields—besides a blazing gallop down the road because she suspected there was work to be done in which she might be included.

Your mule can be used in a variety of situations other than hot pursuit. It can loiter in the shade of a tree or by a gate or water trough. One of my most popular narrative scenes involves an aged mule and elderly farmer enjoying a leisurely retirement. For more excitement in the carving, this mule can be quite refractory, all set to kick someone or thing to kingdom come. Raise her head, shift her weight to the dotted foreleg; her hind leg's already cocked. Look out!

Archival photos at your local library or historical society are an invaluable resource, as are the participants in rural livestock auctions and rural trading days, if you don't remember from your own experience or family folklore. If you have not driven a horse or mule, do some vital research so the tangle of leatherwork that harnesses the animal to the vehicle or implement begins to sort itself out. Arm yourself with a photocopy of a harnessed horse from an encyclopedia or book about horses. You may also want to seek out someone in your area, perhaps by way of an agricultural extension office, who drove, or perhaps still does, and can show you what the prevailing fashion was in your locale. You will then be able to add to your pattern where extra wood will be needed, especially for the collar and hames around the animal's neck; these had many local variations. I harnessed the patterns with my neighbors' equipment, the driving horse in my own light buggy har-

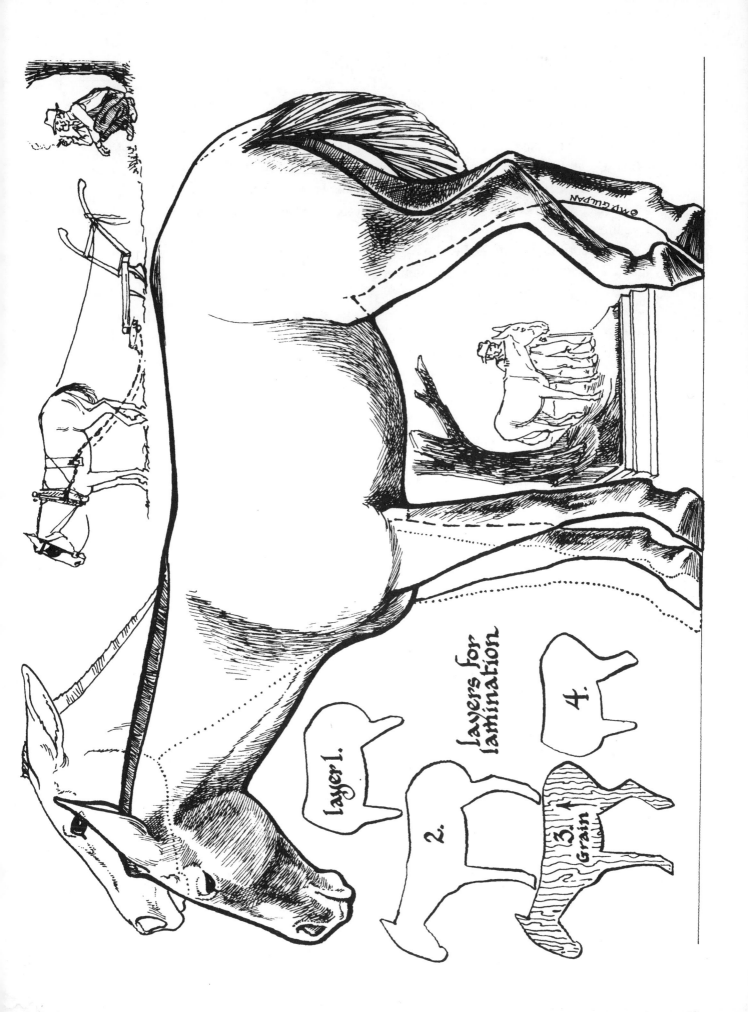

ness, and included my grandfather's mares as token heavy horses.

As archival photos attest, draft horses in actual use were not the size and splendor of the Belgian stallions I rode behind when I was a child. My grandfather's grey Percheron mares were imported at considerable trouble and expense from Indiana into an area where the only pedigreed horses were under saddle or between the shafts of a sulky. Evidently they were considered an extravagant oddity; mules could work harder on less feed, so we'll carve the mule.

1. Be sure to have amended the pattern and blank to allow for harness, or none if your mule is recalcitrant or, perhaps, retired.

2. Now, pencil the front and back views of the mule onto the blank. Note on the sides where extra wood is to be left for the harness or tack, as needed. It is helpful to locate the hooves on the bottom of the blank, quite probably the only time you'll enjoy this kind of impunity while messing around with a mule's feet.

3. Let's carve! Outfitted with your largest ball-nosed burr mounted in your Foredom or your largest AutoMach gouge, establish the peak formed by the mule's hips and backbone. Note that a loitering mule has a tilted pelvis; the weight-bearing leg forces its hip up, while the leg dangling in relaxation causes the other hip to drop.

Next, work up the pyramid shape formed by the tailhead and backbone to either hip; that spare angularity of the rump is characteristic of mules.

Now, get rid of a little of waste on either side of the hindquarters, down to the thighs. They're flatter than a horse's, but remember to leave some tail brush space. Also, watch out for the slight projection of the stifle, that joint similar to a human knee, protruding beyond the barrel on the relaxed side. I used to take hold of our mule's knee and would swing it back and forth against her flank, watching her whole leg flop, pivoting on that tiptoe until she'd anchor it by shifting her weight onto it, switching her tail in annoyance.

Mules have a more sharply peaked backbone than a horse, so as you "rough" your way forward, defining the back and barrel, keep that egg-shape point uppermost in mind. The relaxed leg compresses the flank a bit, pushing a little of the weight toward the opposite side.

4. Check the small scale dorsal view against your own progress here to be sure you are narrowing the barrel as you head toward the shoulders. Those shoulders should be quite lean and considerably more upright than a saddlehorse's, with only the slightest step at the withers where the shoulder merges with the back.

The neck is likewise spare and does not arch at the crest as a horse's does. If allowed to grow, the mane will flop to one side, horse-like, though it is usually roached off completely to keep it from tangling in the reins or harness.

Remove a little of the waste to narrow the sides of the head slightly.

5. A change of tools is now in order; use a taper burr or your smallest AutoMach gouge. We've got the legs to do.

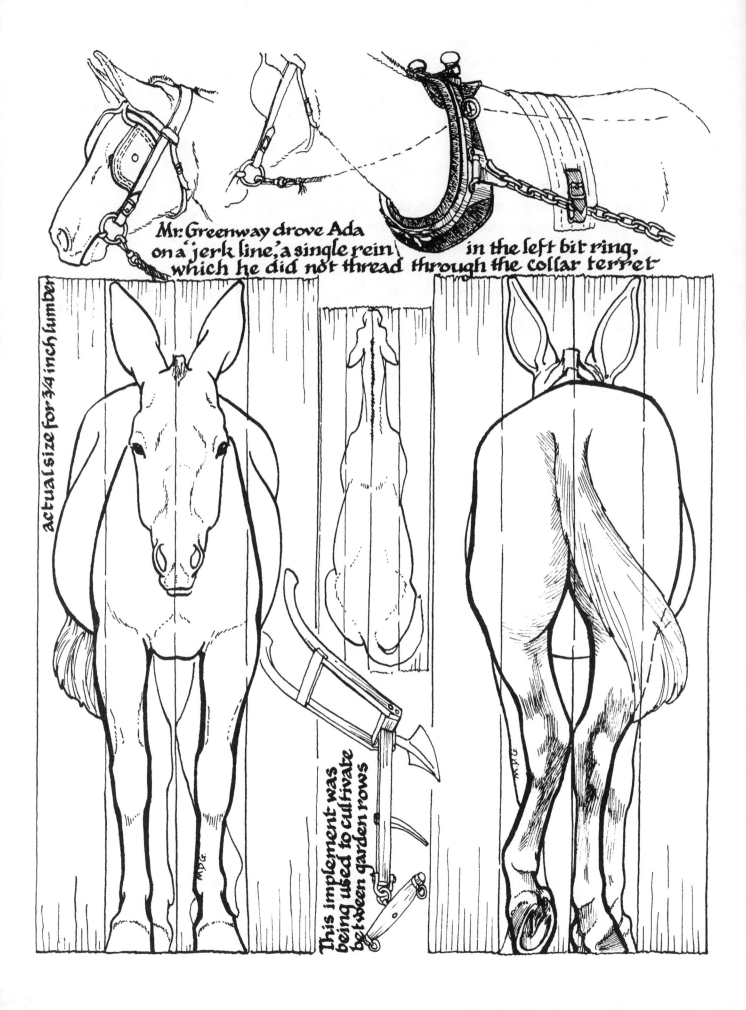

Mr. Greenway drove Ada on a 'jerk line,' a single rein in the left bit ring, which he did not thread through the collar terret

actual size for 3/4 inch lumber

This implement was being used to cultivate between garden rows

Start between the hind feet, from the back, clearing that space to profile that opening. Leave the legs quite square for the time being, concentrating on waste removal to clear the opening. Clear the area between the thighs, then profile the outsides of the hind legs.

There is more waste between the forelegs; start cautiously between the hooves, working toward the chest. Try cutting a long trough from hoof to chest, front, then back. Gradually deepening it until it's cut through is less stressful on the wood (and yourself) than nibbling straight through, cutting at right angles to the leg direction.

6. By this time, the character of your mule should be readily recognizable, so let's attend to some particulars. You might want to switch to a dovetail cutter, if you have one, though a taper burr or your smallest AutoMach gouge will also work here. Start at the head; mules' faces are more coarsely modeled than horses', so don't dither over a multitude of defined facial muscles. Carve the little hollows on each side of the bridge of the nose, cheeks, and jaws.

Start separating and shaping the ears.

Cut the hollow behind the jaws, on either side of the throat, as well as the little ridge that forms the root of the mane. There should be a pronounced ridge where the neck and shoulder meet.

7. Shape the legs next; the fronts of both fore and hind legs are rounded, flattening slightly on the sides and narrowing over the tendons in back. The joints are smaller and neater than a horse's, and the hooves are narrow, more oval.

There are small hollows where the legs join the body, behind the elbows, and in front of the stifles.

8. In shaping the legs, you've probably cleared much of the waste away from the tail already, so all it will be needing is a little refinement. Around here, mules often have the hair clipped off the top of their tails, with the remainder "banged" at hock length, to make them easier to harness, so the pattern is designed for this. You need not completely undercut the tail behind the rump, if it seems too fragile. Just get a nice flowing sweep suggesting motion.

9. Tackle the detailing. AutoMach gouges leave a handsome finished surface that will require only a few chisel strokes to knock off distracting high points. Abrasives, such as sanding drums or cartridge rolls will follow up burrs to do the final modeling. Pencil plan the features.

Eyelids can be incised with the corners of a small gouge; use the tip of a small knife to whittle the eyeball into shape.

The tip of that small knife will model the lips best if used to cut from the mouth corners to meet in the middle. In moments of extreme relaxation, the mule's lower lip will droop until a little pocket forms beneath the upper lip. If the lip is not too frail, cut that little gap. I used to stick my finger in there for our mule to mumble around until it was pretty well slobbered. Another interesting phenomenon was to twiddle that fold inside her nos-

Layer3

Layer2

Layer1
Grain

Layers for lamination...add material to
accomodate your type of harness

This project can
be adapted to
make a second
figure for a team

trils until she snorted gustily. Doesn't that sound like a hot Sunday afternoon in July, and a little child with nothing to do but keep clean until the company came?

Hollow the nostrils with a tiny sphere burr, which can also finish thinning the outside edges, especially at the bottom.

Insides of ears can be hollowed with the tip of your smallest taper burr, followed by a reaming with that tiny sphere employed in nostril clearing.

That same small sphere or a tiny engraving cutter (shaped like a miniature dovetail) will detail the sole of the cocked hoof.

Use your smallest gouge to texture the mane and tail, with directional cuts approximating the lay of the hair. Accent sparingly with a few cuts of a V-tool. Curb your enthusiasm with that rascal; too many parallel cuts of the V-tool cause distracting harsh shadows, turning the hair to corduroy!

Now, except for the smell and the horseflies, you should have a decent mule!

10. Generally, if used as the focus in a setting involving other elements, such as a tree, gate or person, your mule is better treated with an all over stain of some subdued dark color. Often a powerful bond formed between the farmer and the mules on which his livelihood depended. If you would like to add the farmer to your setting, use the pattern from the cow and calf chapter, but separating Mr. John from his grandson and opening his hand, angling the fingers upward to rest on the animal. It is appropriate to finish him in a solid color stain compatible with his mule. In *The Crop's Laid By,* I combined the characteristics of three elderly neighbors in the figure of the aged farmer who has retired his last mule in the uncharacteristically spendthrift way I'd observed many of these gentlemen continuing to feed and pasture idled veteran animals. The man is stained burnt-umber; the mule raw umber—appropriate "earth" colors.

Feel free to paint your mule in technicolor if you like. Most mules have cream colored muzzles and eyelids, with light hair on their bellies and inside the upper legs, both fore and hind. Sorrel, a bright red-brown, with a flax, or blond, mane and tail is a very popular combination, though a good many mules are various shades of dark brown, with black mane and tails, and black on their lower legs.

Now all that's lacking is for your mule to have a good wallow in the dust down in the back pasture as soon as you turn her loose. The old traders in the know say her value goes up 50 cents each time the mule rolls completely over—means that rascal's fat and sassy. Hope yours is a high dollar one!

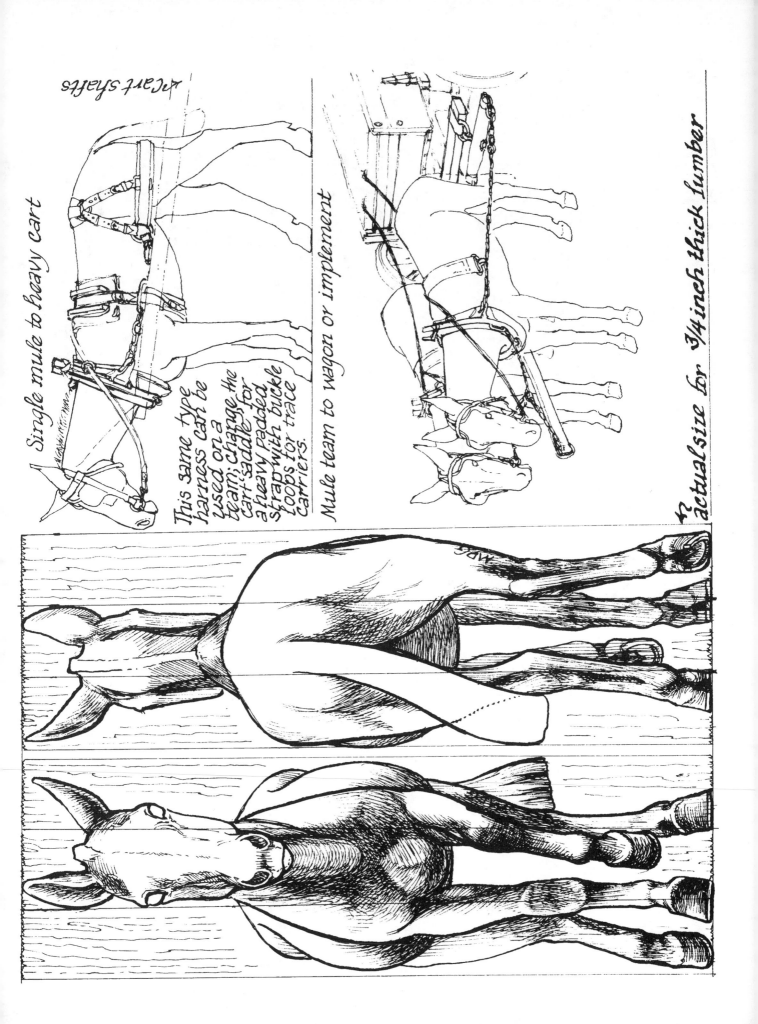

Cart shafts

Single mule to heavy cart

This same type harness can be used on a team; change the cart saddle for a heavy padded strap with buckle loops for trace carriers.

Mule team to wagon or implement

actual size for ¾ inch thick lumber

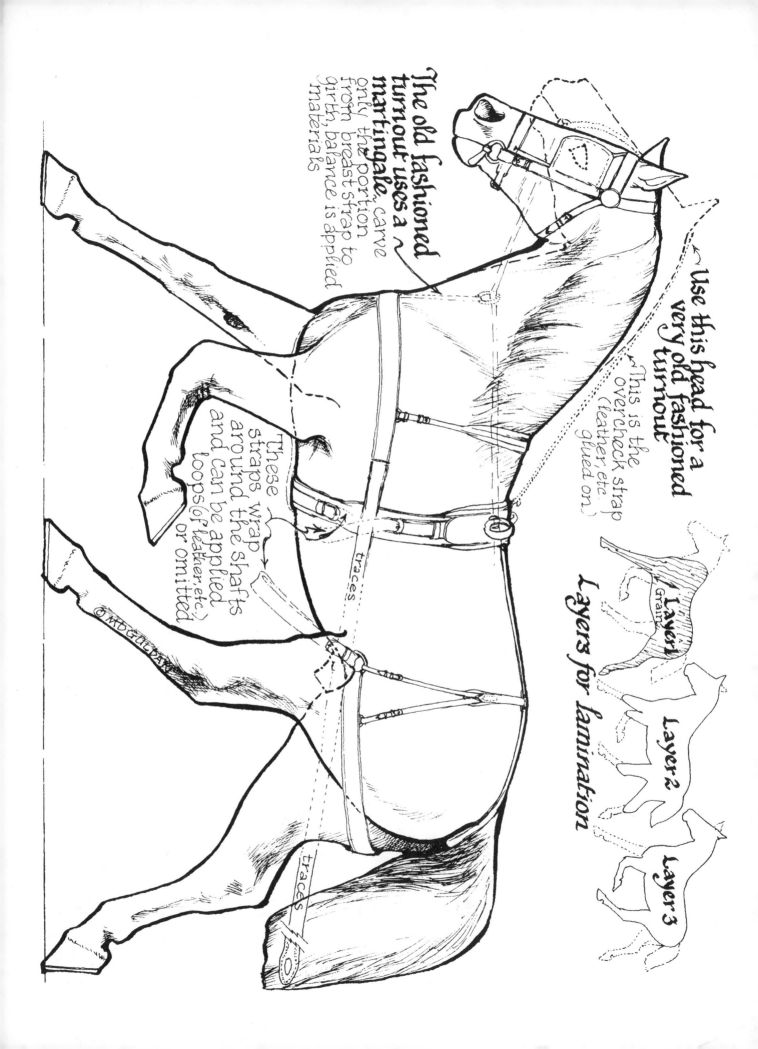

The old fashioned turnout uses a martingale. carve only the portion from breast strap to girth, balance is applied materials

Use this head for a very old fashioned turnout

This is the overcheck strap (leather, etc glued on.)

These straps wrap around the shafts and can be applied loops (of leather, etc.) or omitted

traces

traces

© MD GULDAN

Layers for lamination

Layer 1
Grain

Layer 2

Layer 3

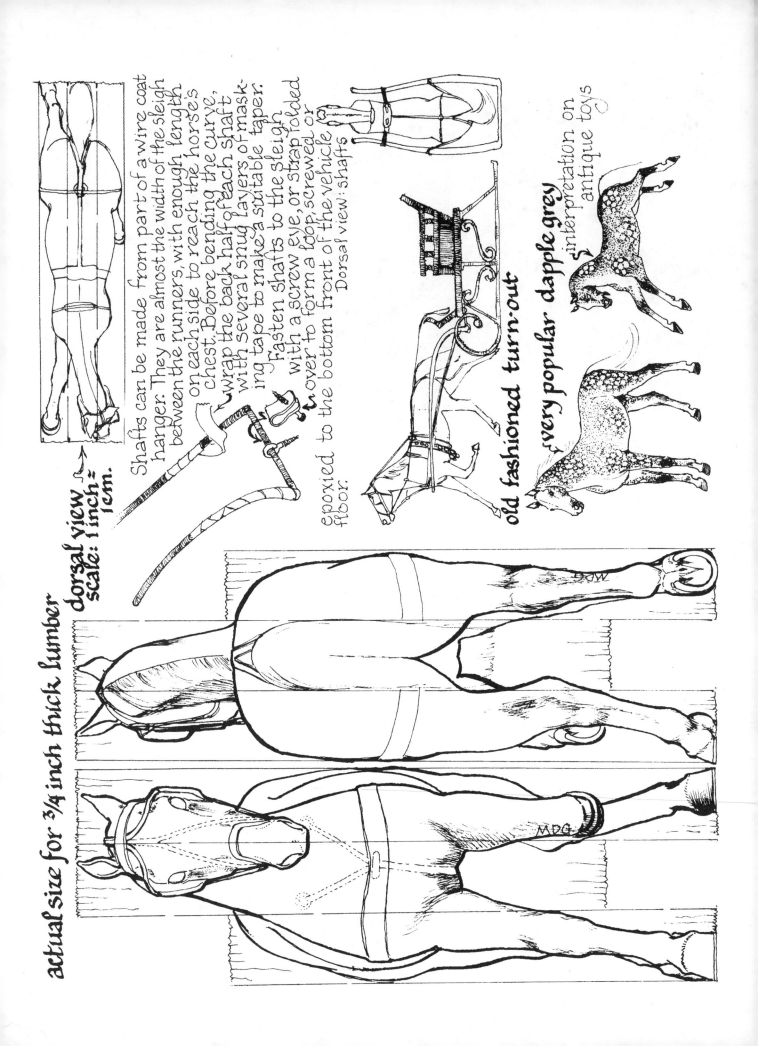

actual size for 3/4 inch thick lumber

dorsal view
scale: 1 inch =
1 cm.

Shafts can be made from part of a wire coat hanger. They are almost the width of the sleigh between the runners, with enough length on each side to reach the horses chest. Before bending the curve, wrap the back half of each shaft with several snug layers of masking tape to make a suitable taper.

Fasten shafts to the sleigh with a screw eye, or strap folded over to form a loop, screwed or epoxied to the bottom front of the vehicle floor.

Dorsal view: shafts

old fashioned turn-out

a very popular dapple grey interpretation on antique toys

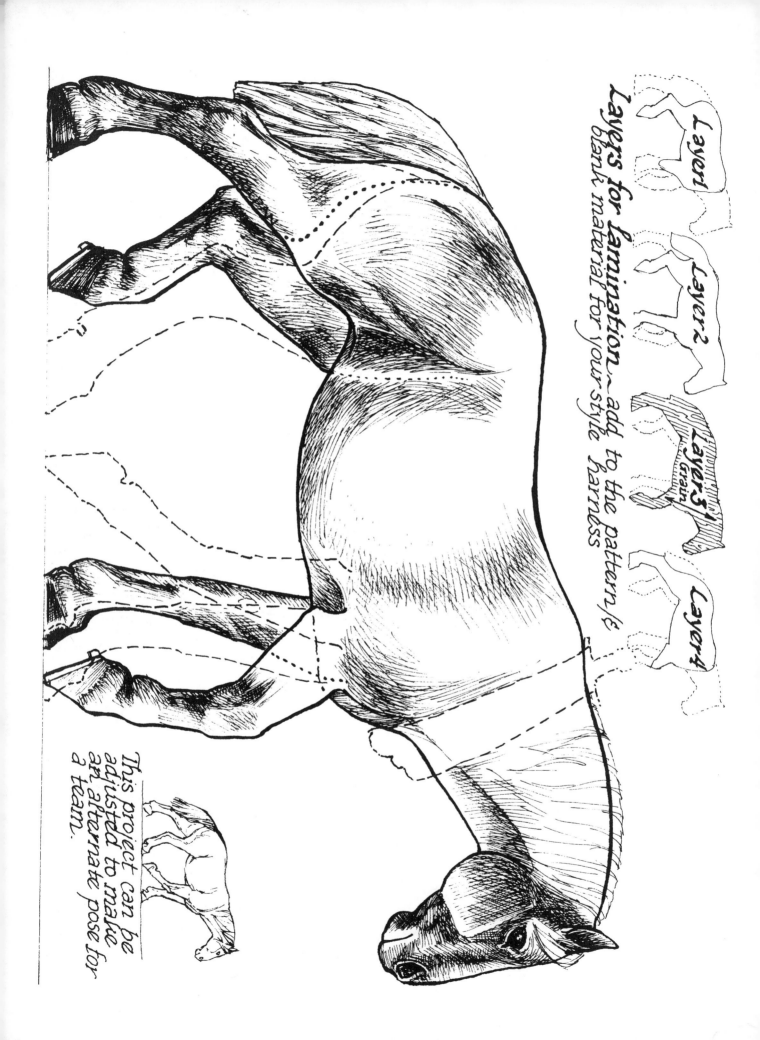

Layers for lamination...add to the pattern/s
blank material for your style harness

Layer 1

Layer 2

Layer 3
Grain

Layer 4

This project can be
adjusted to make
an alternate pose for
a team.

actual size for ¾ inch thick lumber (dorsal view: 1cm. = 1 inch)

Grey Percheron ~ some grey horses become lighter with age...

Human scale: proportionate sizes of a 6ft. farmer, this mare and a mule

Calks added for traction

hind fore
horse hoof prints
mule

draft horse shod

Cow with Calf, Grandpa and Grandson

PANSY and Daisy, the doe-eyed Jerseys my grandfather milked when I was very small, are a vague recollection. But rugged, shaggy Old Red, his last milk cow, had tremendous character, in lieu of pedigree, and will make a fine figure to carve.

Old Red had a legendary tolerance for interference from assorted small grandchildren, who would tumble about underfoot like so many puppies, trying to "help," or who would sit on her hard back to keep out of the way while my grandfather milked and sang.

He always milked enough to fill a tuna-fish can first for Tom, the grey cat, who materialized from out of the hay overhead as soon as his libation was placed on the edge of the loft floor. Occasionally, Paw-Paw would wow us by aiming a squirt into the cat's open mouth as he meowed from his perch on the beam overhead!

Cows are currently a very popular decorative motif—gift shops and catalogs are full of them. You might want to use the cow alone or as part of a tableau with someone milking her, for example. She and the calf make an eloquent and likely counterpoint to the carvings of portrait figures, such as my neighbor taking his toddling grandchild out to see the animals.

Remember that the cow can be done in a smoothly stylized fashion, brightly painted (the black and white Holstein pattern seems to be quite in vogue) and perhaps mounted on a playful base with wheels in the manner of an antique pull-toy for a clever and sophisticated decorator item.

Because of the calf's small size, it is not advisable to carve her with an AutoMach due to the obvious likelihood of cutting one's fingers. Using a Foredom mounted with burrs and abrasives to grind her into shape is better, though with experience, one can certainly whittle the little rascal into proper form with a good carving knife. She can be carved nursing enthusiastically or sniffing curiously as she is approached by the toddler.

Let's get this project underway! In sawing pieces for the cow, it's best not to drill or saw that opening between the leg and tail in the third piece, or it will be too fragile. The opening was included in the diagram just to show which layer included the tail. Leave the calf's tail firmly fastened to the back of the leg, top and bottom.

The cow can be carved with horns or without. Just lengthening her horns will not turn this dairy shorthorn-type cow into a western longhorn. Check your encyclopedia; longhorns have longer, bonier legs and rangier bodies, rather tucked up and narrow through the loin. One of the most characteristic differences is the shape of their steeply peaked backbone at the shoulders and tailhead. There are also noticeable differences in

½ dorsal view, actual size for ¾ in. lumber

adjust teat for nursing calf

Layer 1.

2.

3.

Grain 4.

Layers for Lamination

© MFOSTLYNN

Cow with Calf, Grandpa and Grandson

the points of the pelvis at hip and rump.

1. Laminate the blank to the required thickness, then pencil in the dorsal view noticing that there will be rather a lot of waste to be removed at the shoulder. Since cattle have "independent suspension" of their ears, you may opt to have only one ear turned back, listening to the calf, while the other ear can listen with attention turned forward, focusing on the approach of the viewer. This ear extends at a right angle to the animal's head, the option dotted in on your left in the front view of the cow. On the blank, at this point, the ear is omitted and will be carved later as a separate insert. Its base will end in a peg that will be plugged into a hole bored at the appropriate site at the back of the cow's head.

Draw on the front view of the forelegs and the back view of the hind legs as a guide to waste removal.

2. Let's carve! Using your AutoMach fitted with its largest gouge or your Foredom grinder with the largest ball-nosed carbide burr, start at the rump, cutting away from either side of the tailhead and sloping very slightly downward toward the hips. Cows have conveniently angular rumps, so continue your efforts here, trimming away the sides of the blanks and making the hindquarters a bit narrower than the barrel. Take a bit of waste off the outsides of the hind legs for easy access.

Now, topside once again, turn your attention to the backbone and barrel. Just ahead of the hip joint, the sides of the lumbar vertebrae extend in a protective shelf that narrows into the back of the rib cage. Below this bony ridge, the soft tissues sag like a hammock. Check the dotted profile line in the rear-view detail (this is a cross section just ahead of the hip joint). Notice that the greatest fullness of the barrel occurs at the bottom. Let's work on that rather pear-like shape.

There is much waste to be removed at the front of the rib cage as the barrel tapers there and the shoulders are appreciably narrower than the hips. If you cut your blank as suggested to minimize waste, the leading edges of the two outside layers occur right at the front of the shoulder, so bevel toward that seam.

Unlike a horse's, the cow's shoulder musculature is quite spartan, so the transition from shoulder to forearm is quite smooth. Go ahead and shape the outsides of the forelegs, though there is little waste there.

Trim some of the waste from the sides of the neck and head.

3. Now, if you are using an AutoMach, you will want to change to the small gouge as we've got tight, picky little areas to do. Foredom users, if you have a dovetail burr (shaped like an inverted cone), this is the perfect occasion to use it; otherwise, a taper burr will do.

Use a pencil to plot in the location of the tail and rump before you begin to trim the tail to size. The dorsal-view diagram will remind you that the bovine rump is narrow and wedge-shaped, with the hind point of the pelvis an obvious feature.

Carefully cut the waste from between the hind legs, working mainly from the back. At this step, leave the legs rather square in actual contour for added support.

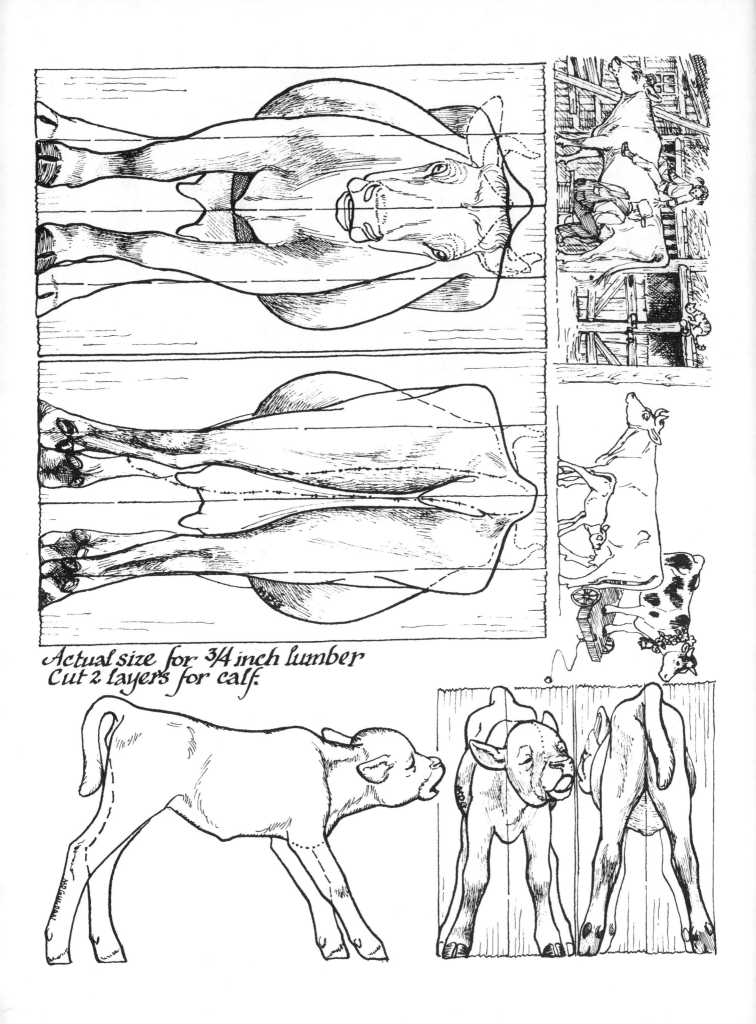

Actual size for 3/4 inch lumber
Cut 2 layers for calf.

Cow with Calf, Grandpa and Grandson

Next, generally indicate the shape of the bag; its four quarters are plump and rounded with a teat at each corner. If you plan to show the calf nursing, remember to fold one teat upward to meet the baby's mouth.

If you have not already done so, indicate that hollow ahead of the hip, where the internal abdominal muscles anchor on the viscera. There is a slight trough ahead of the hind leg, formed by the bundled leg muscles meeting the back edge of the barrel. Surplus skin, which allows leg movement, hangs in a bit of a fold at a right angle to the leg at the stifle joint where the leg emerges from the body. Hollow beneath this a little, forming a distinct belly from which the bag dangles.

Your dovetail burr, if it is a large one, may not fit there easily, so change to your taper, which you'll be needing anyway in order to remove the waste from the knee to hoof. Next work upward, toward the chest. Remember to preserve the dewlap, that fold of tissue at the bottom of the throat from the jaw to its insertion behind the forelegs.

The pectoral muscles, between the forearms, are full and rounded, with the dewlap forming a little central keel.

Don't miss the bucked-in angle of the knees when viewed head-on (and evident in the hocks, when seen from behind); it is characteristic of cattle, though it is a serious fault if it occurs in horses, causing them to strike or step on the heels of their own forefeet when moving at speed. Since, historically, cattle depended on their horns and not their speedy get-away for self-defense, having their sharp edged hooves stepping closer together caused them to cut up less of their grazing ground underfoot when following regular little trails to the choice spots.

4. Let's give more character to the neck and head. Pencil in the location of the ear, if it is not to be an insert, so that you can begin to clear the waste between the ear and neck. At the back of the skull, the first cervical (atlas) vertebra has flaring projections out each side, causing a corresponding bump in the muscles near the top of the neck. Where an inserted ear is planned, this bump is significant. Because of the projection of the atlas vertebra it isn't necessary to clear the back of the ear all the way to its root. Trench enough to cause a strong shadow at the top and bottom of the ear.

The neck is otherwise quite slab-sided, with a ridge along the top and the folds of the dewlap along the bottom.

Since they will be so fragile, let's leave the horns alone for now, save for the clearance around the base required for access to the ear.

The bovine face is quite angular. From the broad, flattened muzzle, the bridge of the nose narrows progressively to its insertion between the eyes. A cross section of the head just in front of the eyes shows the shape of a triangle with rounded corners. The bridge of the nose is the peak with the bars of the jaw at the triangle's base.

Cows do not have the prominent cheek muscles characteristic of horses; the curved and wrinkled brow ridges are their distinctive features. Old Red's eyebrows were furrowed into myriad little creases, giving her the air of perpetual harassed worry, especially when she was dithering over her frolicsome calf of the season.

5. Your are now far enough along to consider the detailing, and the face is a good place to begin. Pencil in the location of the eyes, checking for not only the anatomically correct position, but also for symmetry when viewed head on. Draw on the lips and nostrils.

Employ your own favorite detailing equipment; my choice on burr-rough shapes is to texture to a finished surface with shaving cuts of a small detailing knife. By cutting in the same direction as natural facial planes, the blade leaves a facetted surface which enhances the angularity of the bovine face.

Incise a stop cut at the bottom edge of the upper lip. Trim the lower lip with a cut at right angles to the stop cut so that a little shelf is formed, simulating the overhanging upper lip. Part the lips slightly in front to have the cow lowing. Old Red always "talked" to her nursing calf. We liked to lean against her on the other side with our ears pressed against her barrel, because it seemed like that's where the rumbling, thunderous humming came from. That was a rural Tennessee approximation of Walkman headphones, I reckon. But I have to admit, I still much prefer the cow. Occasionally the calf's enthusiastic butting threatened to tip Red over on top of us, but even scrambling out of the way was fun.

A tiny sphere burr in your Foredom grinder is the best nostril-reamer. After the nostrils are sufficiently hollowed, shave from under their outside lower edges to give them character.

A small gouge works well to stop cut around the eyeballs. Rock it slightly deeper into the corners of the eyes. It may be used to shape the eyeballs if the tool's inside curve approximates the curve of the eyes fairly closely; otherwise, shave the eyes into shape with the tip of your detailing knife. Use the knife's tip to cut in the tear ducts at the corners of the lids.

6. Before we tackle the horns and ears, let's get the legs more nearly finished. For safety's sake, it's better to do this bit with a Foredom. I use a very small dovetail burr; a taper also works well. However, there is no accounting for daring, so tackle this task with the tool that will leave your fingers intact.

The forelegs are rounded along the front, narrow behind, with small, rounded joints. We'll leave them more substantial on the carving than they are on live animals to forestall breakage. A pair of dewclaws project at the back of each fetlock joint, above the hoof. These need not be completely undercut as long as there is enough of a trench cut beneath them to cause a strong shadow. Shape the outside walls of the hooves; they form a long oval when viewed from the soles. Let's leave the cleft between the digits until all four legs are ready.

You didn't forget the little hollow behind the elbows, did you?

Now, let's take care of the hind quarters. If you didn't completely undercut the tail earlier, do that now. Beneath the tailhead, the folded vulva extends below the rear points of the pelvis, so no need to undercut there. Instead, shape the back edges of the hams and sandwich the bag between them. The cow's hind legs are rather flattened on the sides, rounded in front, narrow in back. The hocks are sort of flat and turn slightly inward when seen from behind. The tendons down the back of the leg, from hock to fetlock, form a little ridge which ends above the dewclaws. Now those and the hooves need your attention.

Finish shaping the teats and bag, though you might want to save the final positioning of the teat for the nursing calf until you have him ready to try it for size.

7. If you've carved your figure with an AutoMach, you already have a nearly finished surface. All that is needed before final detailing is just a once-over with your chisel blade to smooth off any distracting ridges left by the gouges.

Figures roughed out with carbide burrs need to have their final modeling done with abrasive drums and cartridge rolls.

Now for the last little detailing. Start with the tassel of the tail. First, refine the back edge of the hock, where the hair brushes it, with the tip of your detailing knife. Then incise a few lines to indicate the clumps of twisted hair.

A little gouge used to make back-to-back cuts will divide the heelbulbs at the back of all four feet. The tip of your knife can remove the chip above that cleft.

With the knife point, scribe between the toe cleats. Use the corner of a small gouge to clear the cleft from each side for a more realistic contour. Be very careful in removing the chip between the toe tips to avoid breakage.

Turn your attention to the ears now. Hollow the inside of the turned-back ear with a tiny taper burr or a small spherical steel cutter. The ear to be inserted is best sawed out with a generous stem several inches long attached to its base. That way it can be easily held while you cut it to shape. Be sure you have made the ear to face the appropriate direction, right side up. Saw off the "stem" and whittle the base of the ear into a peg which can be plugged into a hole drilled in the back of the cow's head at the appropriate site.

The horns are stressed least if cut to shape with a very small abrasive drum used in a Foredom run at slow speed. First shape the outside contours of both horns; then shape the inside curves. Carvers of songbirds sometimes stabilize fragile bird beaks by applications of cyanoacrylate (Super-type) glue, which penetrates and hardens quickly. That technique is beneficial here.

8. If your plans include a calf, this little fellow is best shaped with a carbide sphere burr on the body, head and outside of the legs. Use a taper on the tail and to clear between the legs.

Abrasive drums and cartridge rolls can be used to do the remaining modeling. Carve in the details with your little knife.

Hollow the calf's mouth with a small steel sphere cutter and check its fit to the teat. Don't worry about an exact fit as long as it's close enough and the calf has all four feet on the ground. When the animals are mounted on their base, a putty mixture of clean sawdust

Cow with Calf, Grandpa and Grandson

from the project stirred with a little carpenter's glue can be poked around the teat and mouth. Use a flat toothpick for a spatula. Any corrections can be made with your knife on the dry filler. Only you will be the wiser.

9. Gouge-textured bases hinting at the roughness of pasture grass are most effective for very naturalistic carvings. Trace around the animals' feet first to insure their good balance, then texture around those places with irregular strokes describing a slight curve from one diagonal corner to the other.

The cow is most secure when pegged in the soles of two hooves, as well as glued to the base. The calf will do fine with just glue.

10. These figures are especially handsome when treated with a rather dark stain, though stylized characters are also fun when brightly painted. Cyanoacrylate reinforced horns will not absorb stain, so you will need a touch of oil or acrylic paint for coverage.

If you would like to complete the scene by adding human figures, samples have been included. My piece is a portrait of a highly respected, very successful local farmer, John Verell, and his first grandchild, Johnny. Since then, Mr. John has had more grandchildren, and his enthusiasm is undiminished, a universal feeling which causes this carving to be recognized everywhere it is displayed.

Despite the size and extent of his reputation, Mr. John is not tall and is very spare and purposeful, so there is a little extra room in this blank where you can make every effort to commemorate a special farmer or grandpa of your own. The techniques can easily be adapted to make the man stand alone, as mentioned in the mule pattern, holding his team with his hand upturned instead of holding his grandchild's hand.

In preparing your blank, you will note that it is three layers thick, a proportion which will still work if you enlarge this $7^1/_2$ inches tall figure to 10 inches for some other project. The shoulder planes would just reach the outside edges of a three-layer blank in that enlargement. A single thickness supplies sufficient material for each arm.

The ubiquitous bill cap has its bill re-instated on the completed figure, and the illusionary brim, which seems to be thinner than it actually is, will prove a useful technique on hat brims of other kinds.

1. When your blank has been constructed pencil in the front and back outlines of the fur. As you would with livestock, begin roughing out by establishing the angle of the trunk leaning toward grandchild/mule. Cut to the outline on the right and left sides, keeping the figure quite squared at this stage.

2. As soon as the trunk has been indicated, work down the legs toward the knees and feet. Most people's legs are slightly offset at the knee. An imaginary line drawn through the center of each joint, then viewed from the front, would not be perfectly straight.

When the outsides of the legs match their drawn outline, separate them, starting at the gap between the feet and working up to the crotch. (Actually, you'll probably find this easier to do if the figure's held upside down.)

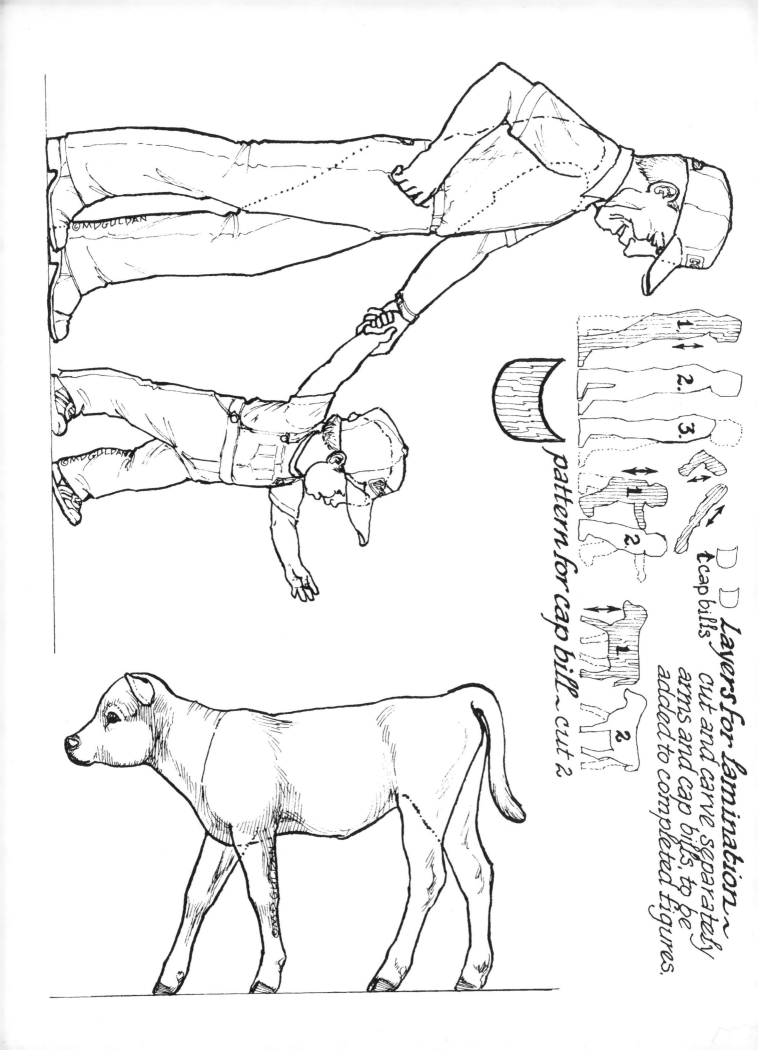

©MDGULDAN

©MDGULDAN

Layers for lamination~
cut and carve separately
arms and cap bills, to be
added to completed figures.

↑ cap bills

1.

2.

3.

1.

2.

1.

2.

pattern for cap bill~ cut 2

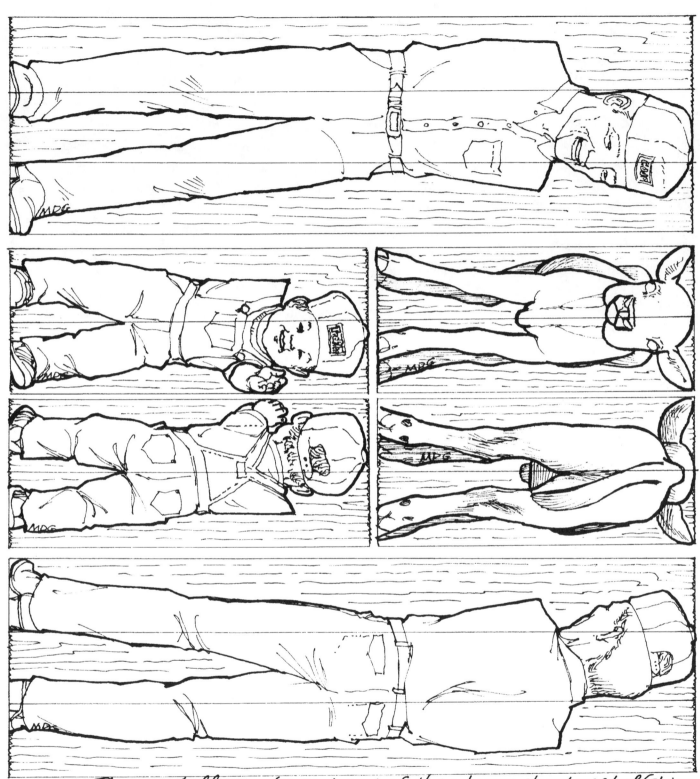

The cap bills can be cut out of thin brass sheet metal (shim stock) with sharp scissors. (Fold a tiny "hem" under, using pliers, around the outside edge to avoid accidental skin cuts.)

However, an illusion of thinness can be carved, by sanding the edges of the bill quite thin, while leaving the interior actually a fairly sturdy wedge where it will be fastened to the cap. (This is the view from underneath.)

3. Decide, next, the direction in which your figure will be looking, and indicate this on your blank, drawing a straight line on the face area corresponding to the line one can imagine going between the eyebrows and straight down the nose.

There's a hefty bit of waste down one side of the head; cut it off, leaving the blank square, gradually matching the front and back outlines. With the waste removed, you may begin rounding out the back of the head, coming to a peak on the nose line you just penciled in. When seen from overhead, the head and face should form a very broad wedge shape in front with quite rounded corners in back.

4. With a change to smaller equipment, let's get the knees to poke out in front, not a whole lot, as we commence rounding the fronts of the thighs from a little peak above each knee. Check your own leg for reference, as the section from knee to foot is slightly peaked down the front and causes the pants to take that same shape. The lower legs are more rounded at the calf, but the tendon anchoring those muscles to the heel makes a little ridge which shows in the soft fold of the clothing.

Whether or not your particular person stands with his toes pointed apart a bit, this is the usual stance and makes your carving easier to balance on its base. Since I usually rough out human figures with a carbide burr in my Foredom, I find it easiest to draw the footprint on the soles of the inverted blank and cut around their outsides until each line is reached, leaving the feet at first quite squared. Then the upper sides of the feet can be rounded over into their characteristic shape.

Since you will have arrived at the tilt of the shoulders when you first roughed out the profile view, the next most significant aspect of the upper body is the hollow down the center of the back formed by the parallel ridges of muscle down both sides of the spine. The hollow is slightly deeper in the small of the back.

That having been established, you can then round the corners of the rib cage, taking care to reserve flat areas at the shoulder sides where the arms will attach.

5. It is best to do all the characterization from this point on with your detailing knife, especially if it has a curved "sabre clip" blade. The blade will automatically cut the curved strokes that simulate soft folds in clothing, as well as the lay of skin over muscle and bone.

Take careful notes of clothing detail actually worn by your subject: where seams are located, button counts, pockets (and any visible contents), belt and buckle, shoes or boots, the way they crease the cap's bill, the cap's emblem.... I take reference photos, as well as notes, but rather than trying to explain about quarter-turns to Mr. John, I stood him out in the beanfield when the crop had just been planted and meant to walk around him, taking pictures from every angle. He was as good humored as always, having been accustomed to these illogical projects and requests. However, he has been around livestock and large equipment too long to ever turn his back on anything, and as I was trying to walk around him to get pictures from all sides, he kept turning to face me! We never did get him to stand still—and that's characteristic, too!

How to arm a man~

First, carve his body, leveling the point of attachment at the shoulder into a flat plane. Complete the feature carving and detailing, just don't add fragile accessories like the cap's bill yet.

Carve and detail the arm from the hand to just above the elbow. Check and double check the fit at the hand's contact point...in this case, with the pocket; eventually, with his grandson.

Now we need to get the shoulder exceptionally flat. Trap the figure on edge, cradled in the folded towel...

(Bricks or thick books caught between blocks clamped to your workbench)

Using a sharp knife with a stiff, straight blade_turned up on edge like a roadgrader or cabinet scraper, scrape across the shoulder, changing direction slightly with every pass. Check your progress constantly_avoid fuzzing the grain by scraping against it. Eventually the place will be smooth, level.

Hold the arm in place; pencil onto its rough shoulder a line matching the angle of the newly-leveled site. Be careful_this can be tricky_check from on top, front and back. (You've heard this old saw_measure twice/cut once!) Use your stiff straight knife of earlier to cut on this line. Hold the arm against a sturdy scrap of wood; slice firmly on the pencil line, removing the waste in one or two cuts. Check the fit at the shoulder.

Whittle a little peg about the size of a kitchen matchstick. Drill a hole, which the peg fits snugly, in the upper arm at a right angle to its attachment surface. With the peg installed, hold the arm to the shoulder so you can mark the spot to drill.

This time, coat the shoulder with glue and peg the arm into place, pivoting it quickly for the most natural pose.

Strap it with a band of masking tape and let it dry before doing the final shoulder shaping.

Cow with Calf, Grandpa and Grandson

If this piece is to be painted, or stained a dark color, using your burning pen on clothing detail can be quite helpful.

Illustrated instructions for installing arms are given, along with a helpful hint on making the cap's bill, which should be glued in place at the very end.

Johnny, the grandson is just a smaller version of the same techniques, with his free arm attached because it's such a small part. Go ahead and prepare and peg the other arm; just pose the two figures together, so that you can carefully mark exactly the angle at which the joined arms meet each figure.

I go on and carve the shoulders pretty much to shape by holding them in place, one at a time, with no glue. When the figures' base is ready, strap them to their arms with tape, temporarily, until their positions on the base can be marked. Human figures are most stable when glued and screwed to the base by a woodscrew inserted from the underside of the base, up into the foot and leg on one leg of each figure. Then quickly glue their arms in place while the glue is wet enough to allow any minor adjustments.

Those boys are too engrossed to go far!

Bulls, Longhorns, Oxen

IF a cow is to calve, replenishing the family's supply of milk and meat, you can be sure there is a bull nearby. This bull occurred in our herd by some confounding genetic quirk, sort of a throwback to the fleet-footed scrub cattle of pioneer times. Because he never got as big as his pedigreed Angus father, he was fast and agile, able to jump any fence in the county. He was the hazard that he looks like, alert and aggressive.

Longhorn cattle, on which the fortunes of western ranches were based, were the gritty survivors of brutal natural selection in their environment. Predators, poor quality forage widely scattered over rugged terrain, and vicious weather weeded out any livestock unable to endure, leaving an angular, spare, rangy animal named for its defense equipment. Both sexes were well armed; however, steers, the sterilized males, grew the longest horns. The longhorn bull here is pawing announcing his intention to fight.

In addition, oxen have been included because theirs was the muscle that moved America. Able to pull a heavier load than horses, and subsist on overnight grazing without the horses' grain rations, oxen, technically steers that were worked, dressed out a meatier carcass if butchered in desperate circumstances.

1. As soon as you've decided how to use this fellow, make up an appropriate blank, noting that ears and horns will be added to the finished body. We will go through the procedures for the first bull, which can easily be modified for the longhorn or oxen.

If you plan to do a yoke of oxen, do each animal separately, without the yoke. The profile pattern you use will allow you to carve bows around the necks of your oxen, which will peg into corresponding holes in the bottom of the yoke. The tops of the bows protruding through the yoke will actually be pegs whittled to the appropriate length and poked into the top of the yoke. This can save you some frustration; through if you have access to the round cane used in craft classes to weave baskets, this can be used to make authentic bows that poke right through the yoke.

2. Especially if you are doing the first bull with his head turned, pencil in a centerline down his back, up over the center of his neck and head, to remind yourself of how his head will be turned. The longhorn is only slightly turned.

Mark the dorsal view carefully on the top of the blank. Mark the outlines on the backs and fronts of the legs as well.

3. Now start roughing out! Use your largest ball-nosed burr or AutoMach gouge and start knocking off the corners of the animal's barrel, working from the point of his hip, forward toward the back of the shoulder blades where the swell of the shoulder begins.

Work on one side, then the other, swapping back and forth frequently to keep the form from getting lopsided.

While a bull's hips are squarer and his whole shoulder girth more uniformly oblong

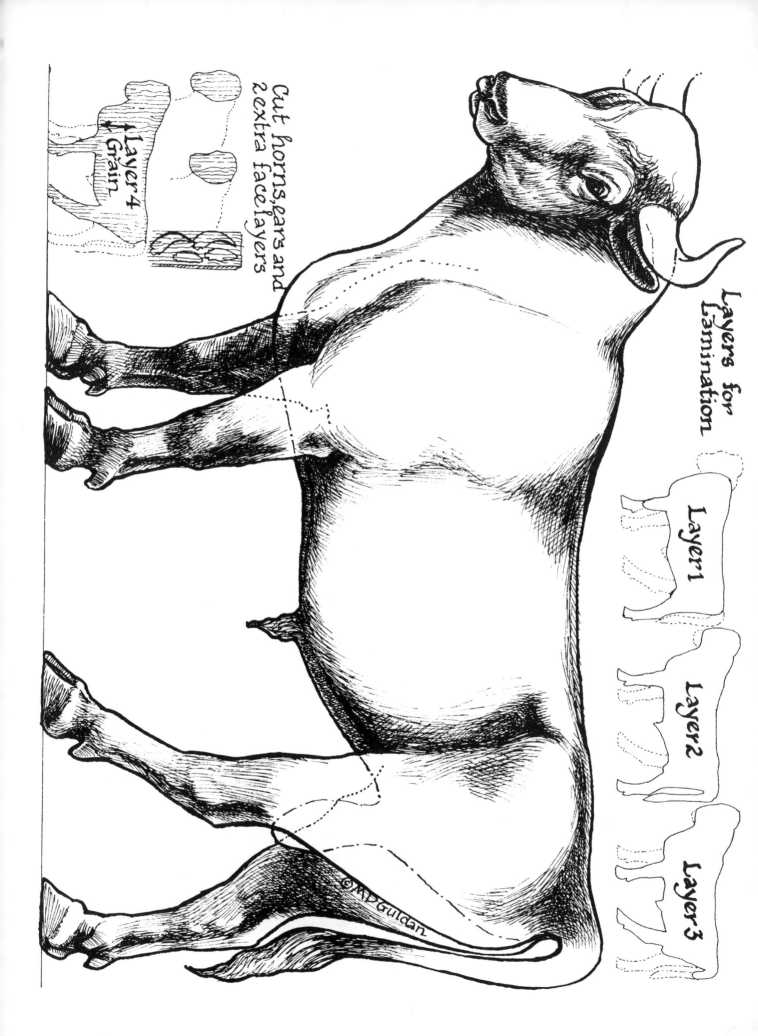

Layers for Lamination

Layer1

Layer2

Layer3

Cut horns, ears and 2 extra face layers

Layer4
↑ Grain

©MPGuldan

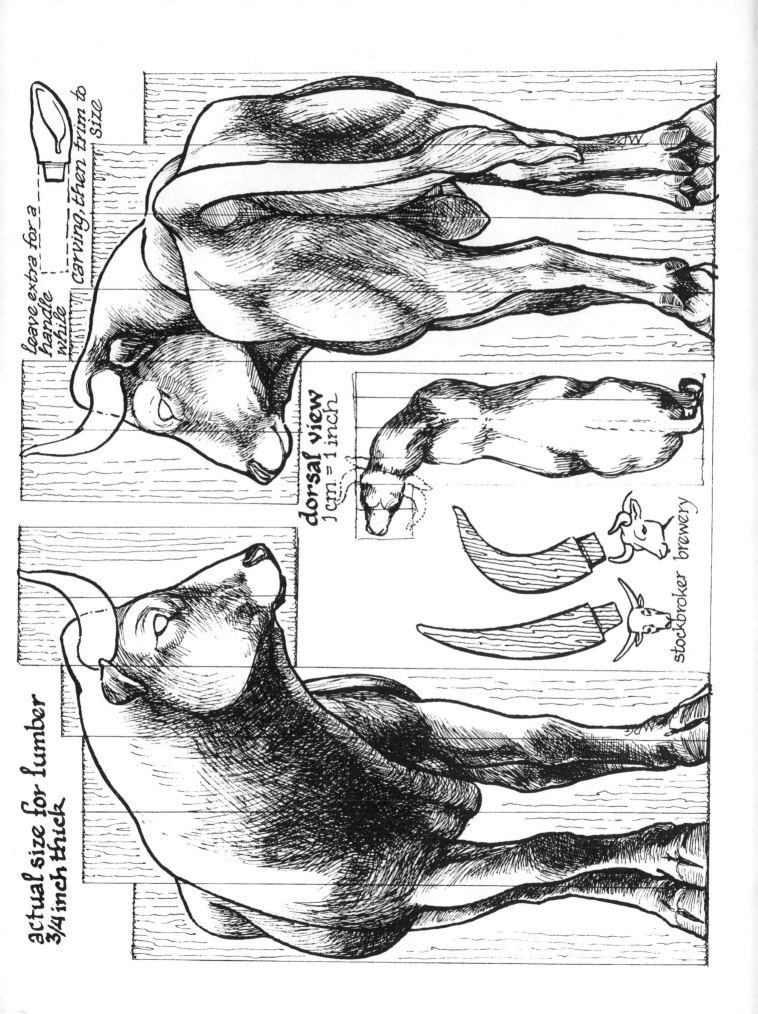

leave extra for a handle while carving, then trim to size

actual size for lumber 3/4 inch thick

dorsal view
1 cm = 1 inch

stockbroker brewery

than a horse (this is because he lacks the muscular development that makes him proficient at leaping or long-distance galloping), his barrel is the same egg shape, slightly narrower at the top and wider at the bottom, as the horse's.

Begin to round off the bottom of his barrel working from back to front, then aim for the slightly narrower top, broader at the bottom overall shape. Remember that a bull's backbone is encased in quite a lot of muscle. It may even appear as a slight furrow between muscle mounds from shoulder blade to hip. It is not a raised ridge like a cow's.

4. Draw in his front face and ear, because the next tactic is going to be to develop the swell of the neck and to define (but not yet undercut) his ear and the side of his face. Start with your large burr or gouge, working on the area from the ear tip toward the cheek. Round off the top of the neck, working from the sides, center, toward the top, back and forth on both sides.

5. Shape up his shoulders, beginning your cuts from the widest part above his forelegs and heading upward on both sides. The masses of muscle should start to flow into one another, from back to shoulder to neck.

6. Now work on the angle of his face, from nose to poll. Next, starting from the chin, work on the long curve of the dewlap under his neck. Note the raised, corded character of this tissue. Your cutting strokes should progress from the shoulder downward, indicating the dewlap with your largest gouge or the BN carbide burr in only general terms, at this point.

7. Round out the bottom contours of his barrel, working from the back toward the front. Give him a little hollow behind the forelegs to accommodate his elbows.

8. With caution, taking off only small bits at a time, start at the hooves, working upward where the wood grain will permit and refine the legs. If you start on the hind legs, you can work your way right on up to the hips, which helps to develop the muscle masses in their proper context. Note that the bull's tailhead is the highest point of an incline beginning between his hip bones.

Keep referring to the front and back views of the legs that you drew onto the blank at the onset. If the legs are rather square at this point in roughing out, it is to your advantage, as it will support them through the refinement of the body with the next blade change.

9. Now, switch to a carbide taper burr or a small gouge, so that you can go to work on the bull's face. His characteristically sinister expression is due to the heavy brow ridges of tissue to protect his eyes in head-to-head combat; you will need to develop these and the taper of his muzzle.

In developing the definite triangular feeling of his head from all views, you will want to cut and undercut the ears on the turned side to get them to actual outside shape. Work from base to tip where possible, then you will have access to the back edge of the jaw, which should be made to curve right on down to the chin.

10. With the smaller taper or gouge, you can define the furrow where the dewlap meets the throat and chest and gradually tapers into his girth in a slight ridge. The contours where his neck meets his shoulder will need clarification. Follow the shoulder muscle down to his forearms and tuck it into his barrel right behind the elbows. There should be a noticeably crowded look on the inside of the turn where the bulk of the neck and shoulder meet.

Clean up the contours of the shoulders, back, and hips, defining muscle tissue as needed and finishing the slope from hip to point of rumps on either side of the tailhead.

11. At this point you will need to develop the cleft where his hams meet. Refine the hind legs by carving in the hollow above the hock joints, the knuckled form of the hocks themselves, and the slight hollow along the lower legs' sides formed by the bone and tendon. Use the small gouge or taper to remove wood between the dewclaws and to shape the ankles. Use the same procedures on the forelegs.

If you are using a gouge, remember that the texture of gouge marks can be left unsanded to form your final surface. If that is the case, make sure that the marks follow muscle masses or hair direction so as to cause no distracting shadows.

12. For the detailing, use whatever tool suits you for each part of the job. Some suggestions are: Shape the tail with a taper burr, working from tassel to tail head where possible to avoid breakage. Your smallest taper burr will best clear the area between the hind legs and scrotum and can give it the pouch-like shape. The taper will also shape the little twisted tassel of hairs at the end of his sheath. While other burr-cut areas will probably need to be sanded, these hair tassels should be left rougher, textured by gouge or burning pen.

The same equipment can be used to texture the coarse and sometimes rather curly hair on the poll between his horns.

A small gouge can stop cut the outlines of his eyes, which are whittled to shape with the tip of your detailing knife. Scribe the wrinkles over his eyes and nip out little slivers to make the folds more pronounced.

Use your burning pen to outline the nostril openings and the lips, which show from the front, but are hidden under the flews on the sides. Use a tiny sphere cutter to hollow the nostrils little by little.

The burning pen, followed by definition with your detail knife, can be used for the refinement of the cleft between the cleats in the front of his hooves and the corresponding division between the heelbulbs in back. It also can be used to shape the dewclaws on the back of the legs above each hoof.

While the longhorn bull does have his ears carved in place against his neck, the others will have ears, as well as horns, carved separately and added later. Since the horns are located higher on the head, let's carve and locate them first.

My big black bull was carved to use a pair of rooster spurs two of my Bantam Old

This project can be done as a steer

Layers for lamination ~ Cut out and carve horns separately.

Grain
Layer 1

Layer 2

Layer 3

Layer 4

©VAUGHRAN

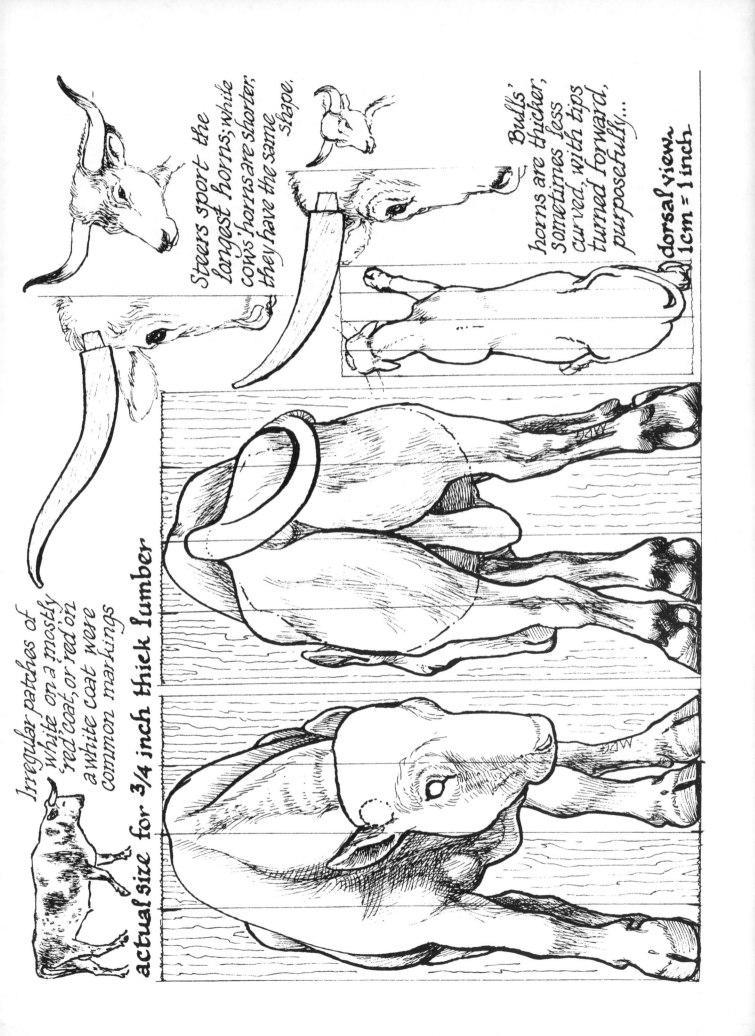

Steers sport the longest horns; while cows' horns are shorter, they have the same shape.

Bulls' horns are thicker, sometimes less curved, with tips turned forward, purposefully...

dorsal view.
1 cm = 1 inch

Irregular patches of white on a mostly 'red' coat, or red on a white coat were common markings

actual size for 3/4 inch thick lumber

Bulls, Longhorns, Oxen

English Gamecocks broke in encounters with kennel wire over the years. Spurs or any horn-type product can be incorporated in the same way that one does carved horns. In carving wooden horns, it helps to leave a handle on the base while you carve the horns to shape. On completion of the carving, trim off the handle, leaving a peg about a fourth of an inch long on the base of the horn.

Mark the drill site carefully on both sides of the bull's head, holding a pencil or pen in place on each mark while you check for symmetry from the front and top. A hole about 3/16 inch in diameter in each horn site will do. Trim the peg to fit the diameter of the hole, and level the base of the horn (a pass with your burning pen can be quite helpful). Test the fit, but do not secure the horns until the ears have been carved and their holes drilled.

That, we shall do immediately. Abrasives or your whittling detail knife can shape the back of the ear, then its outside edges. The burning pen can outline its opening; do your hollowing with the little sphere cutter, but not so enthusiastically that you get any part too thin. A tiny taper burr can refine the hollow toward the flaring outside edge.

Make sure as you go to work on the next ear that they will form a pair!

When the ears have been shaped, they will be attached just like the horns (which need to be safely removed as you begin to drill).

Do a dry run with ears and horns in place to check their fit before gluing them permanently.

13. Now color... Here's the recipe for ebonized wood:

Squeeze from tubes of artists' oil paints: one inch of black, 3/4 inch of raw umber, and 1/2 inch of prussian blue. Mix these together with enough Watco Danish Oil Finish (natural) or some other varnish-based turpentine solvent wood finish to a sloppy liquid. Place your carving atop lots of newspapers to catch the considerable mess you are about to make and apply the mixture generously to the whole piece.

Monitor closely to guard against drips, resaturating porous areas that absorb the stain quite quickly. Fix up more of the color mixture as needed. It is best if the piece is not completely even in color.

Follow the finish manufacturer's directions in regard to subsequent coats. Using Watco Danish Oil, an excellent stain occurs with three applications of stain. They recommend a 30-minute wait, then wiping off any wet, shiny spots with a clean, dry, lint-free rag.

After 72 hours, this finish can be safely waxed, if you like.

14. For technicolor pieces, photos show all white, as well as solid black, red (burnt sienna, sort of a rusty red-brown), and cream-colored animals. Spotted animals are shown in the pattern details. When you go out in the pre-dawn to round up your help, you look for white markings which show up in low light.

Animals with light colors usually had whitish horns with dark tips and dirty tan, light-colored hooves.

15. While you already know how to go about yoking your oxen, let's mention some particulars. At the bottom of the yoke is a large iron ring to which the implement, vehicle or load was fastened. Why not bend this out of brass wire, making its fastener (the "steeple" as staples were called around here) out of wire as well. Poke it into a little hole drilled to size in the yoke. Do not permanently fix the yoke in place until the oxen have been fastened to their base.

Our neighbor logged with oxen, using a pole truck. The heavy iron wheels were chained to the front of a smaller diameter log less than 16 inches across. A pole truck was used on high, dry ground to keep the log from gouging into the ground when dragged. Steve and I used our wheels this spring when an ice storm felled the utility pole down to the barn. The beleaguered utility company couldn't get to the pole, so with a little antique technology, we did it ourselves.

Mr. Taylor's oxdrawn harrow, made of 8-inch square oak timbers all morticed together, with large, square iron spikes to break the soil, was as wide as the yoke. The operator stood on top of this fearsome grid, shifting his weight to keep the implement level. One of the oxen wore a ring through a hole pierced in his nose. A line, secured to the ring and passed up over the horns and yoke, was held by the operator, and used, I gathered, like the jerk line on a single mule. A long, firm staff with a pointed end was used to reinforce voice commands directing starting, stopping, and right and left turns. Teamsters driving multiple yokes hitched to heavy freight wagons or large logs never seemed to use nose rings or lines. They usually used a bull whip with a short wooden handle, a long braided leather lash, and a cotton cord popper on the end in place of the goad.

The front wheels on these vehicles, before there were paved roads, were about four or five feet tall to cope with the holes and the rough roads; some of the back wheels were even larger in diameter. Check the height of the wheels on the cannon displayed in public parks for an interesting view.

Now you're in business, but without the flies and cowpats.

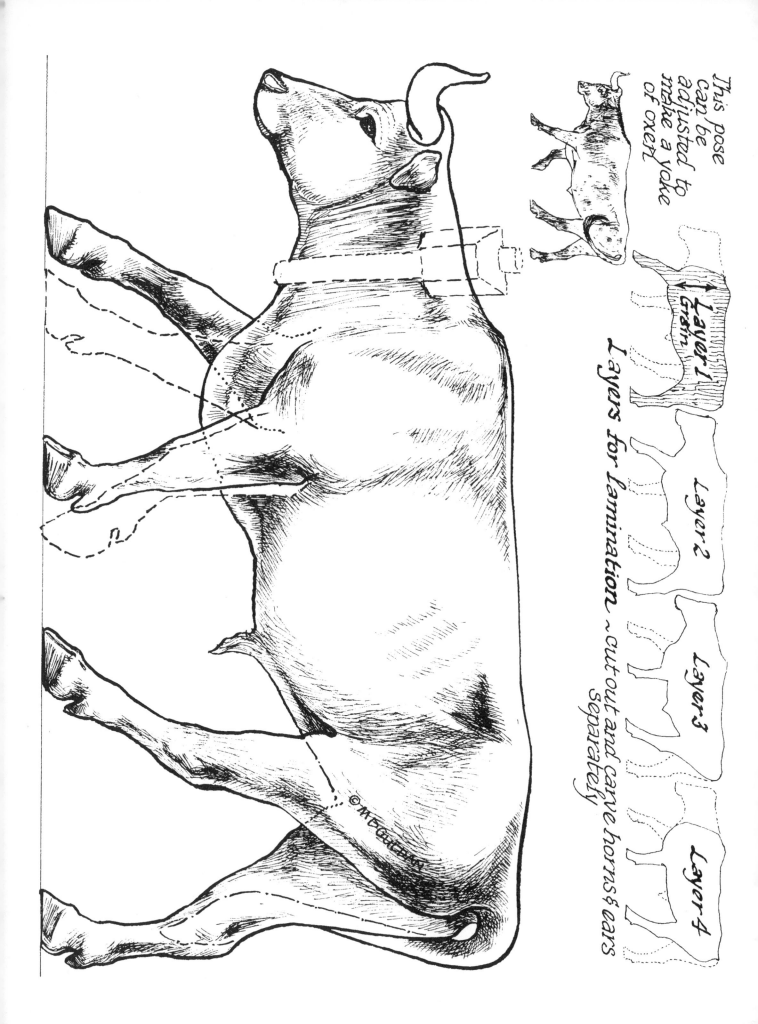

This pose can be adjusted to make a yoke of oxen

Layer 1
Grain

Layers for lamination ~ cut out and carve horns & ears separately

Layer 2

Layer 3

Layer 4

©M.B.Cushman

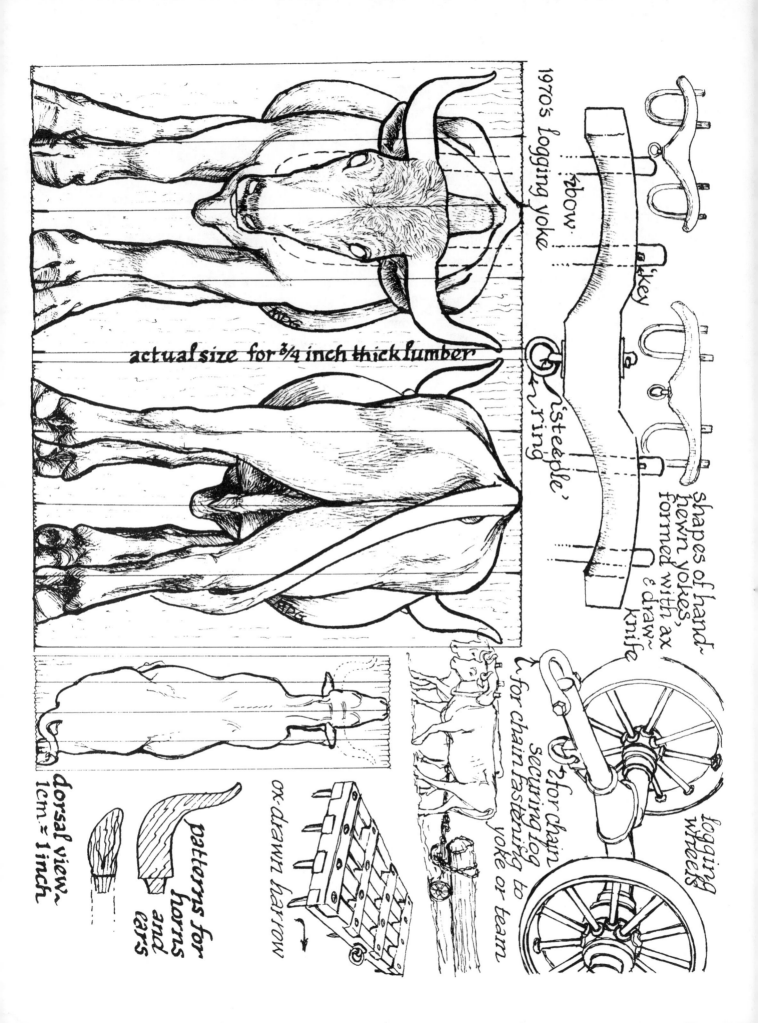

1970's logging yoke

'bow.

'key.

actual size for ¾ inch thick lumber

'steeple' ring

shapes of hand-
hewn yokes,
formed with ax
& draw knife

? for chain
securing log
for chain fastening to
yoke or team

logging wheels

dorsal view~
1cm ≈ 1inch

patterns for
horns
and
ears

ox-drawn harrow

Bobcat

IF you've stumbled through some of our hoofed animals, the bobcat is going to seem like a vacation. He is pictured in summer pelage, because during this season his fur is such a gorgeous red-brown color, freckled with tiny dots like a miniature leopard. Actually, the bobcat's physique conjures up a closer kinship with the power-packed forelegs of the pre-historic saber-toothed tiger, which also seems to have had that curiously abbreviated tail.

Decide on your cat's pose; if you'd rather he snarl, transpose the front face view on the neck and shoulders instead of the profile. As you saw layers for your blank, include that projecting ear in Layer 3 and two additional face-shaped layers to stack on top of Layer 4.

1. When your blank has been assembled and you've penciled on the dorsal view and locations from front and back for all four legs, consider this anatomical point. You'll see in the front and back views that this animal is so muscular that the backbone is buried in a shallow furrow at the shoulders and hips. The bobcat's muscles continue to bulge almost to the base of his tail and forward to the back edge of his rib cage. Only from there to the point of attachment at the back of his shoulder muscles is his back more rounded.

Now, use your largest ball-nosed burr or biggest gouge and start roughing out your cat. Begin right over the bulge of his hips, rounding and, at the same time, tapering his rump toward his tail. Check your rear view; let your strokes start at that extended knee joint and work toward the top of the hip to establish the tension of the crouched position.

Let's get rid of more big waste. Memorize the taper of the rib cage when seen from above—big in back, narrow in front—and start hewing away waste to get that. The back edge of the shoulder muscle extends pretty far on the front of the rib cage, so when you arrive there, make the shoulder bulge gradually widen.

By now, you've arrived at the bump over the top of the shoulder blades. Before tackling the considerable waste alongside the neck and head, shape the forelegs a little. Starting at the widest point—the elbow on one side, wrist on the other—work your way toward the shoulders and back, allowing bulges for the muscles in the forearms. The shapes should flow into each other, suggesting lithe movements.

2. Now, be careful of your cat's ears! Starting at the back of them, narrow the neck. Bobcats, like other cats have very large bunchy jaw muscles, but in addition, they've also got very large ruffs of hair there, too. The neck is short, rather sharply defined by the fronts of the very mobile shoulders (see the Dorsal View), and the back edge of the jaw ruff. The top of the neck is wide at the atlas vertebra right behind the head and narrows a bit on its way to insertion between the shoulders. Further down the neck, the muscles that raise and lower the head are a fairly constant thickness from top to bottom, determining the extent of the little pipeline you see in the dorsal view.

3. For now, leave the fragile ears alone, but pencil a muzzle-sized oval on the front of

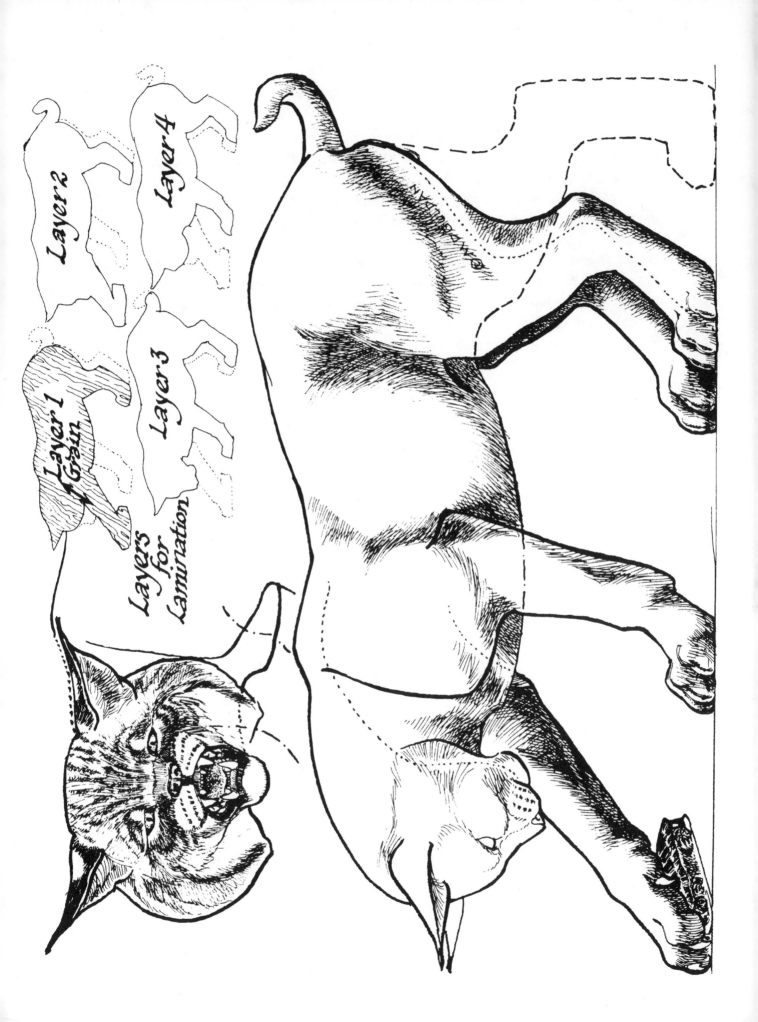

Layer 2

Layer 4

Layer 1
Grain

Layer 3

Layers
for
Lamination

Bobcat

the blank. Start at the back flare of the ruff, first removing the stepped edges of the outside layers of the blank. Gradually you will form a smooth transition from ruff to muzzle, rounded over the forehead and more peaked over the bridge of the nose. You'll notice a sort of boxy projection of the muzzle and that the chin comes to a rounded point.

4. While you were cautious about working around the face, you can relax and strip off the waste remaining on the outsides of the legs, starting with the hind legs. When the outsides of the legs have met your profile pencil line, do the insides, leaving them quite square at first. Once the waste is removed from outside your outline, then begin to shape the legs. Round paws have decided knuckles; fronts of legs are more rounded; and the backs of the legs are more narrow, with knobby little heels and well-defined joints at the hock.

When the bulk of this waste is out of the way you will have better access to the barrel, which is rounded along the belly just ahead of the hind legs. Between the forelegs, it has a decided keel in front.

Cats, like deer, derive much of their tremendous leaping prowess from the elasticity of the tissues strapping their shoulders to their ribs. The shoulder blade and upper forearm form a little shelf-like edge, standing up away from the neck.

5. That turtle being investigated should be trimmed to an oval shape, best done from underneath.

Now begin to shape the bobcat's ears by cutting between them first. Then gradually form their pyramid shape in back, leaving the tips a bit thick for safety.

It is safer for the cat's tail, as well as for your fingers, to shape it with a sphere burr and not a blade. Develop its little u-shaped quirk from the outside first. Change to a taper to trim the inside of the curve into shape. The genital area is just like a domestic tom's and can be defined, along with the cleft between the hams, with a small dovetail burr.

6. Since this is such a sinuous, sleek body, why not consider this for your finished surface: refine face, paws, and turtle first with knife or shallow fishtail gouge, stop cut with the burning pen, knife tip cutting little slivers from beside claws and between toes and shaping eyeballs—you get the idea.

7. Having done those fiddly bits, next use abrasives for your final sculpting. Start with a coarser grit and caution, and shape the fluid body so that the form flows fairly smoothly. Change to finer abrasives to clean up and define muscles; your equipment will do some lovely soft-edged furrows between muscle masses. Blend the larger areas of the face and feet that you blade-textured into the satiny hide.

The ears should be hollowed just a little from the front with their edges sanded quite thin from the back. There is a characteristic tuft of hair elongating the tip of each ear to a little point. Be especially careful that you don't crush those ear tufts when you turn the cat up to finish his tail. We tilted the grain to make this little tail less perilously fragile, but it is amazingly small when compared to the other appendages!

8. Now that you've carved this handsome little hunter, you just want to sit there

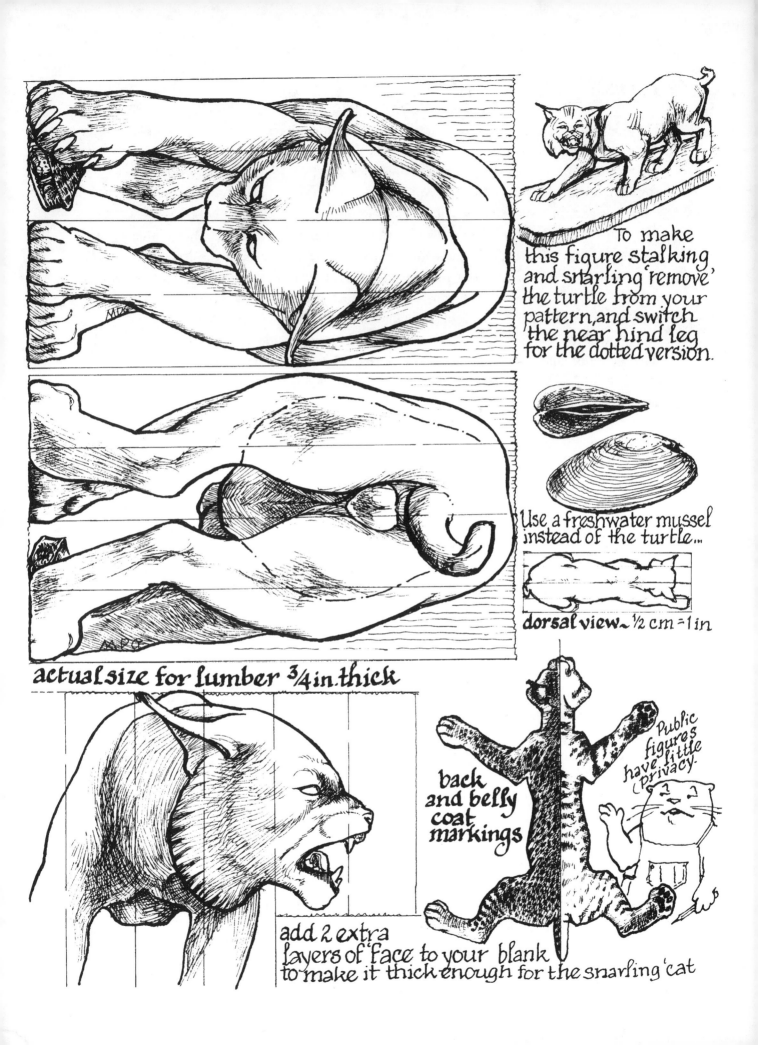

To make
this figure stalking
and snarling 'remove'
the turtle from your
pattern, and switch
the near hind leg
for the dotted version.

Use a freshwater mussel
instead of the turtle...

dorsal view ~ ½ cm = 1 in

actual size for lumber ¾ in. thick

back
and belly
coat
markings

Public
figures
have little
privacy.

add 2 extra
layers of 'face to your blank
to make it thick enough for the snarling 'cat

breathing deeply, admiring your creation. The last thing you want to think about is painting several zillion little polka dots!

Even if you are not accustomed to doing so, seal this figure with the type of sealer compatible with your favorite paint. Yes, the type for acrylic does feel like you're painting on plastic and may make basswood look sort of pink, but it will work out for the best.

The underside base coat needs to be done first and allowed to dry thoroughly. Use a creamy mixture of raw sienna and white with a touch of yellow oxide or ochre. Using the belly coat marking diagram as a guide, paint generously from muzzle to tail tip. Check the snarly cat face to see where the light patches appear around the eyes, muzzle, edges of the ruff, and inside the ears. The light patch on the back of the ears is white.

When this has dried completely, put on the rufous topside. Cut burnt sienna just a little with the medium or mixing agent appropriate to your color and paint the topside of your cat liberally. Use a frayed old brush to pull the color down onto the edges of the light areas. This is going to need to dry completely.

While it does, paint a scrap of wood with leftover body color so you can practice dappling. Since the scrap is unprimed, it should dry pretty quickly. Check the back coat diagram and, using a small, soft, nearly dry brush and undiluted burnt sienna, try making a patch of little oblong dots, very transparently painted. If your body coat turned out a little dark and the dapples don't show, try mixing a very small amount of burnt umber (a darker reddish-brown) into your burnt sienna. This you will use for the dots and stripe pattern shown in the back markings. It needs to dry thoroughly before any other color is added.

At such time, use straight burnt umber and an almost dry brush for the stripes, dots and smoky paws shown in the belly diagram.

When this has dried, mix a little black with the burnt umber for a brownish-black. Use it to outline the nose, and to paint the lips, whisker dots, dark cheek stripes, eyelids, and backs of the ears. While the extended claws are usually pale and white, their sheath openings often have a dark line. Use this color on the turtle.

For the bobcat's nose, use burnt sienna, a little red, and enough white to make a dark brownish-pink. For his eyes, mix burnt sienna with a warm yellow. Their elliptical black pupils can be carefully painted on once the eyes have dried. Even if you plan to finish his eyes with a coat of clear gloss, still give each of them a white dot highlight beside the top right of the pupil slit.

When you paint the white patches onto the backs of the bobcat's ears, also add some dry brushstrokes of white to his light-colored tail fur.

If you are feeling confident, add whisker bristles located on each side of the muzzle in the dots and a couple of eyebrow hairs over each eye. If you've got a very small drill, poke the little holes, or punch them with a strong sewing needle. Install whiskers snipped from a sash-and-trim brush. They can be held in tweezers and dipped in glue before insertion.

Caribou, Ambling Elk

THIS piece will be an excellent exercise in carving a long-legged grazer, and another excuse for some really rich color. Barren Ground, or Peary's caribou, are a pale, creamy version of this long distant traveler with the incredible antlers and amazingly large hooves. The woodland caribou are a mixture of silvery white and walnut dark brown that make an eye-catching display piece. As is true of the other big-antlered deer, caribou must gain as much weight as possible to see them through the rigors of the frenzied breeding season. We'll picture this bull at his peak; big and fat and shiny. We'll give the elk's coat his own chapter.

For this fellow and the walking elk as well, you'll notice the ears and antlers, like the ears and horns of the bulls, are carved and added separately.

1. Since this is such a straight-forward pose, your carving is going to be remarkably streamlined.When your blank has been constructed and your guidelines drawn, start at the widest point of the hips and work back toward the tail, hewing from the sides of the rump to get the characteristic wedge shape when seen from above. Having done that, round over the top of the hips as you see in the back view and continue right to the rear.

Next, there's the round, fat barrel, wide at the back, wedging in behind the shoulder blades in front. If you've become proficient enough, instead of cutting straight up and down the sides until the outline is reached and then rounding, visualize that backbone (the center glue seam) as your goal, and begin rounding from the center of each side. There should be only the least suggestion of a high point along the backbone.

While you're at it, go on rounding those corners in the other direction. While it's quite fully curved along the back of the belly, the front of the rib cage narrows into a sort of oblong shape, squeezed in between the forelegs.

Both elk and caribou advertise their condition with great weight gains in the shoulder and neck area. So as you cut up over the tops of their shoulders, make the curves generous and the neck thick.

Follow the shape of the neck right into the head, aiming for a broad wedge shape, tapered at the muzzle. Both of these animals have sort of broad, bovine noses when compared to the white-tailed deer.

Both caribou and elk have a ruff of thick, long hair down the underside of the neck. The elk's mane tapers a bit more; the caribou's is generous and full.

2. Now, go back to trim the waste from the outsides of the legs, but this time, don't take your earlier shortcut of rounding immediately. Cut the legs square first, concentrating on the angle formed between the body and the hock and knee joints, and then from those joints to the hoof.

While it may look like the caribou is sloshing about on out-sized spatulas, his habitat

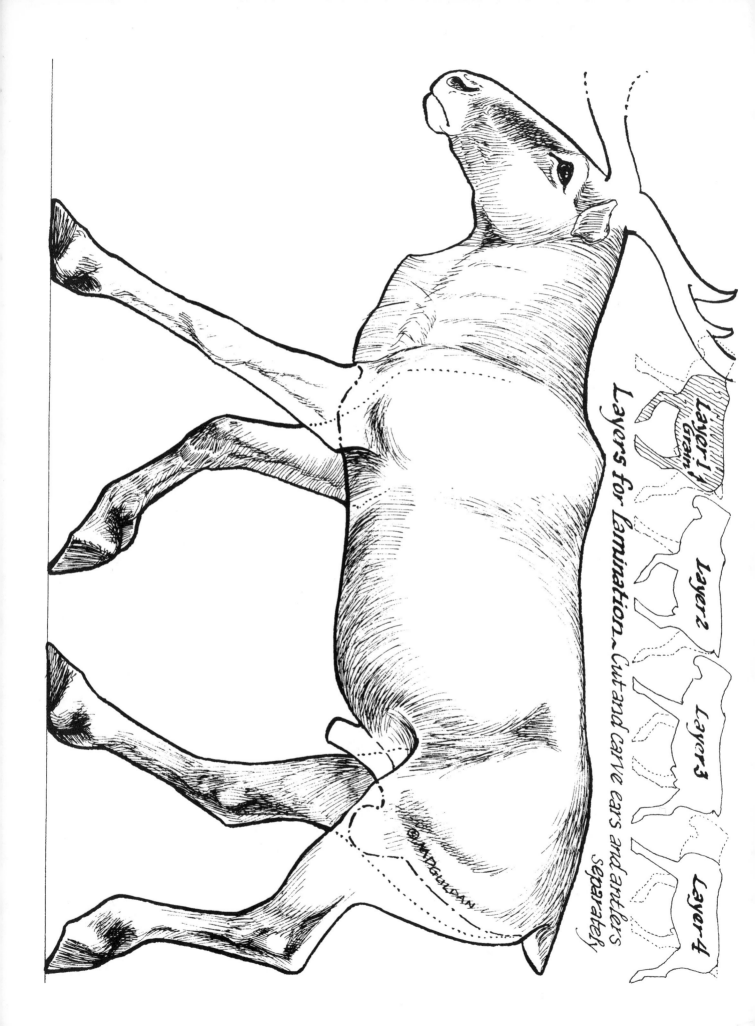

Layer 1
Grain

Layer 2

Layer 3

Layer 4

Layers for lamination. Cut and carve ears and antlers separately

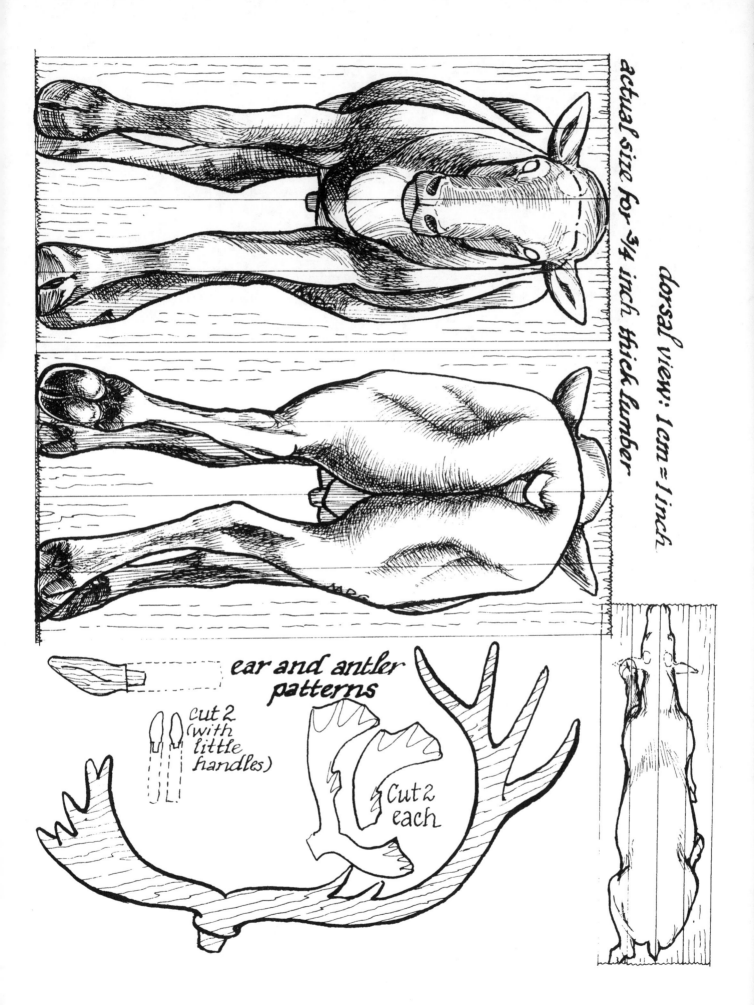

actual size for 3/4 inch thick lumber

dorsal view: 1 cm = 1 inch

ear and antler patterns

cut 2 (with little handles)

Cut 2 each

Caribou and Ambling Elk

encompasses a lot of spongy, boggy, or frozen ground. His broad hooves and prominent dewclaws spread to keep him from sinking and also give him his name, meaning "digger," for the way he paws snow away in order to graze. These formidable hooves (fortunately for us) have a fringe of hair between the cleats, so as you trim the insides of the legs to conform to your guideline, treat these feet like Clydesdale hooves. Leave them as single units for now.

3. When the legs have been roughed out, change to smaller tools to shape them. As with the legs of the mule and cattle, they are more rounded across the front and more peaked down the back with the dewclaws fanning out above the hooves like inverted y's. The hooves flare from a little shelf-like coronet band right at the edge of the hairline.

A little tiny sphere burr or cutter or a very small gouge are best for clearing the small hollow between the heelbulbs and dewclaws on the back of each hoof. These same tools can do the trick in shaping the sheath and scrotum.

4. Both of these animals have angular bony faces, with a pronounced brow ridge over the eyes and a rather broad, flattened forehead that narrows abruptly at the bridge of the nose. The jaws are only slightly narrower than the forehead, with strong, broad cheeks like horses, mules and cattle. Their muzzles tend to be a bit squared when seen from the front and, in both animals, the edges of the lower jaw are overlapped at the mouth by thicker upper lips. In both animals as well, the start of the mane forms a little ridge between the lower jaw's sides.

5. Now, do the same detailing for these well-stocked animals as you did to show the sleek shine of the bobcat's fur. You might want to do the detailing now and sculpt the rest of the body with abrasives. Use your detailing knife to plane the bony face, outlining the nostrils and lips with your burning pen. The lips can be shown by removing a sliver from beside the burned line with your knife tip. Use a small sphere cutter to hollow the nostrils.

Stop cut the eye outlines with a little gouge, shaving the eyeballs to shape with your detailing knife. Then use the knife to cut the slot-like opening of the lachrymal gland at the front of the eye.

Hooves and dewclaws can be stop cut with your burning pen, but resist the temptation to cut too deep a cleft, making these areas too fragile. Cut just enough of a trench to make a shadow, it can be enhanced with dark paint later!

6. The rest of this plump body can be done with abrasives, so that muscle furrows and body hollows will have gentle contours and look fully larded.

With a small diameter cartridge roll you can add a few slight ripples to the loose hair of the mane and accent it with texture lines from your burning pen.

7. Inserting ears was described in carving the bull, should you need to refer to that technique. Specific instructions for antlers are given here. They are best cut to shape using the Foredom. The completed antlers are pegged into holes drilled in the animal's head. Check the fit carefully before gluing them into place.

8. Now that long-awaited caribou color can be put on! In water-based paints there is a silvery blue-grey, Paynes Grey, that will be ideal, if handled with care. A dot of that and a dot of raw umber added to white make a pale, smoky silvery white that will go on first. Use it on the very front of the muzzle, outlining the nostrils, on the cheeks and neck, on the inside of the ears, on all four legs from above the hooves up the backs, in a stripe down each side, and on the back of the rump. All this needs to dry thoroughly.

On the barrel and from the knees and hocks, up each leg, use raw umber tempered with only enough burnt umber to keep it from looking greenish. You are looking for a rich, dark, oiled walnut color.

For the face and lower legs, mix some Paynes Grey into the body mixture to get a shade darker brown. This can be used on the hooves and dewclaws.

When this has dried thoroughly paint his eyes black. Add white in the genital area, on the back of the rump, and on the underside of the tail. Drybrush some white on his mane and into the hair above his hooves. By then, his eyes should have dried enough to place a tiny dot of white highlight in each.

The antlers should look like polished bone. Make them white, tempered with a little raw umber. They should be lighter on the tips of the tines, with a little darker staining on the beams.

Now, there's a splendid animal!

Woodland Caribou

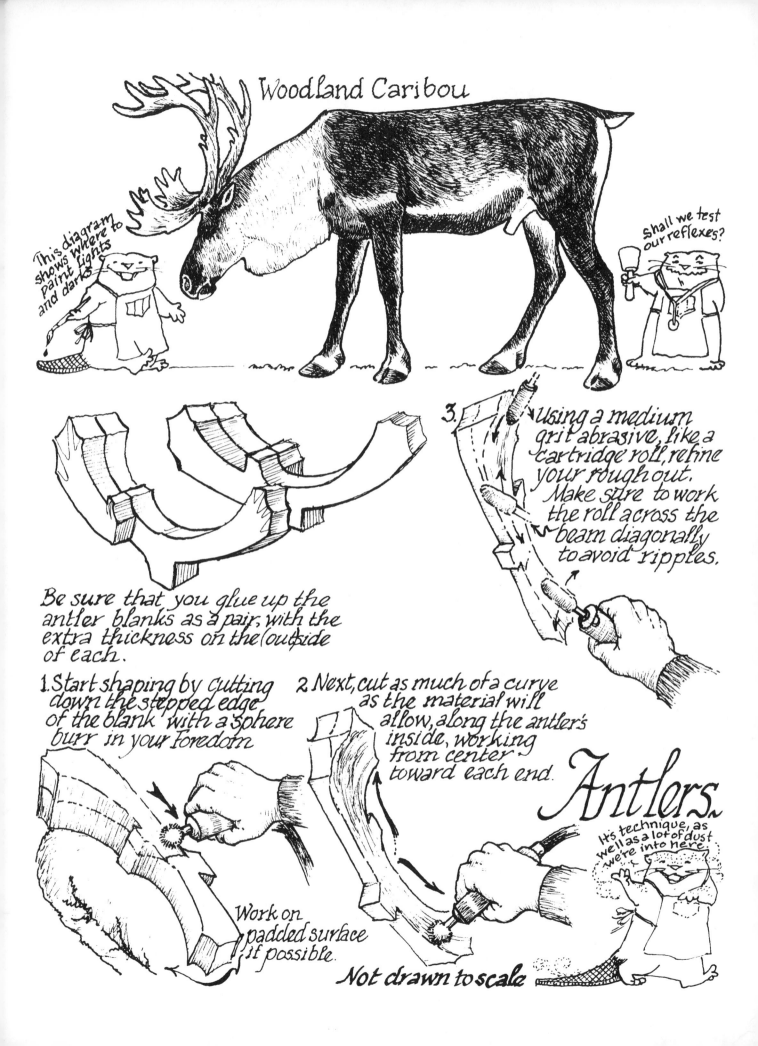

This diagram shows where to paint lights and darks

Shall we test our reflexes?

Be sure that you glue up the antler blanks as a pair, with the extra thickness on the (outside of each.

3. Using a medium grit abrasive, like a cartridge roll, refine your rough out. Make sure to work the roll across the beam diagonally to avoid ripples.

1. Start shaping by cutting down the stepped edge of the blank with a Sphere burr in your Foredom

2. Next, cut as much of a curve as the material will allow, along the antler's inside, working from center toward each end.

Antlers

It's technique, as well as a lot of dust we're into here.

Work on padded surface if possible.

Not drawn to scale

4. Now, turn the antlers over.

Using either the abrasives, if you have found your wood to be a little fragile, or the sphere burr, cut the corresponding curve to match your first effort. Work from the center toward the outside edges...very gently. Gradually taper the collected tine ends into wedges.

So far, we've left the beams quite squared. Take your pencil and plot the location of the tines.

(Even though the antlers on the live caribou aren't that symetrical, we'll make ours match, it's less confusing.)

5.

If this piece is to be colored, so the char won't show, if you've got a burning pen, use it to make the stop cuts at the tips of the tines. (The char hardens them.)

With your smallest taper burr, start at the top of the gap to open between the tines, and cut down from each side to form a little "valley," by degrees.

6. Back to the abrasives! With a small, medium grit cartridge roll, clean up the little "valleys." Gradually sharpen the points of the tines. Then, cut bevels along the edges of the beams. These are rounded little by little, as is the base. The stopcut for the anchor peg can be done (carefully!) with the burning pen. The peg is then sanded or whittled to size. Done! (sigh of relief!)

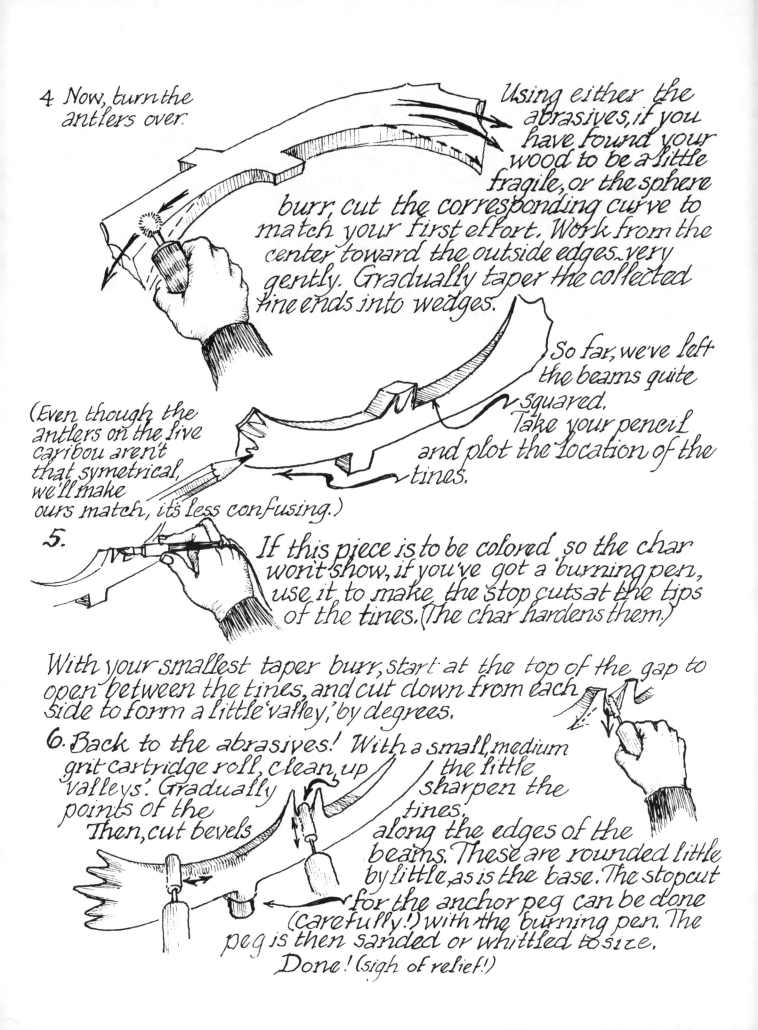

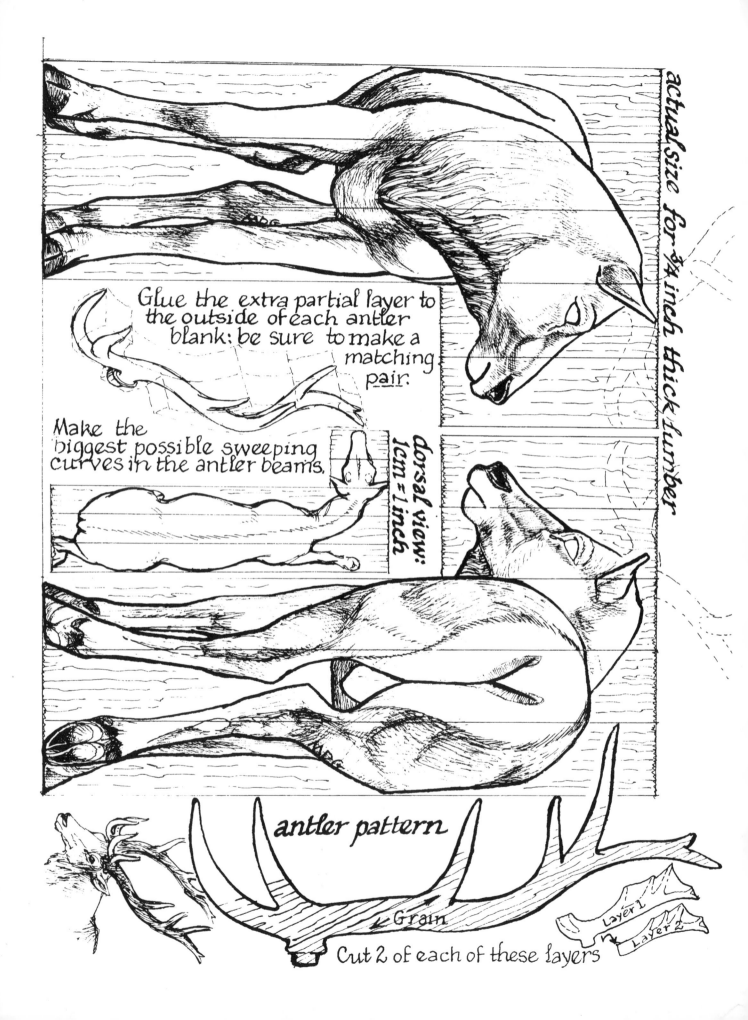

Glue the extra partial layer to the outside of each antler blank; be sure to make a matching pair.

Make the biggest possible sweeping curves in the antler beams.

dorsal view: 1cm = 1 inch

antler pattern

Grain

Cut 2 of each of these layers

Layer 1

Layer 2

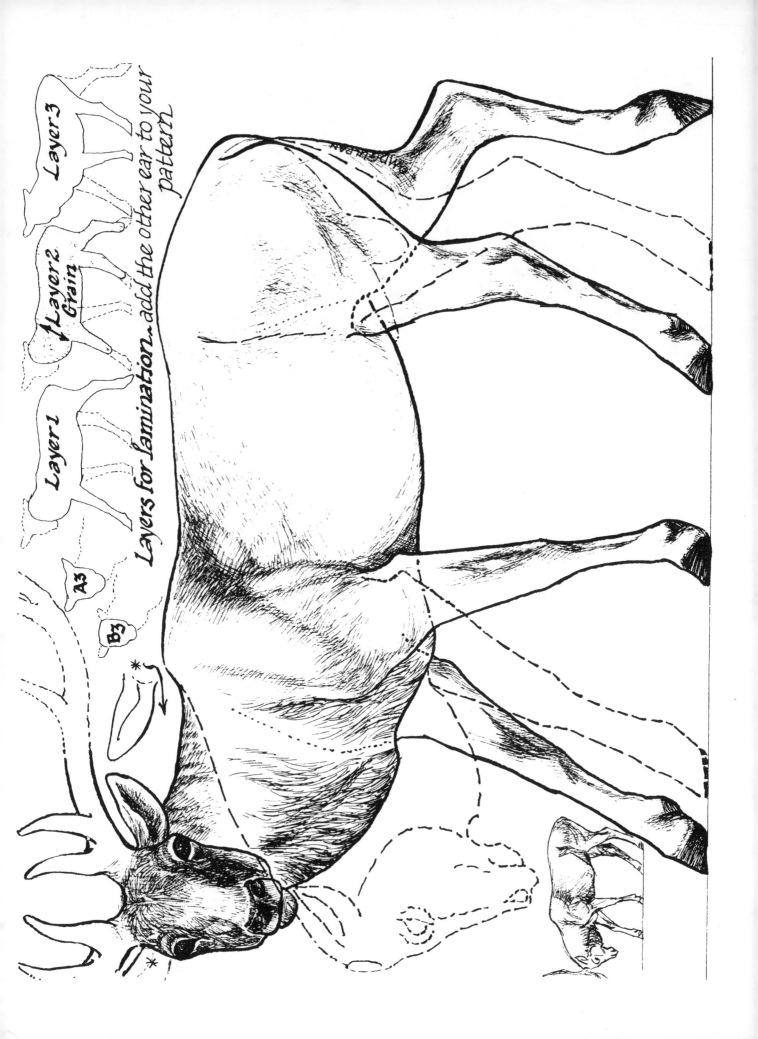

Layer 3

Layer 2 Grain

Layer 1

Layers for lamination.. add the other ear to your pattern

A3

B3

Dead Elk

THE real challenge here is to make this elk look really dead! As there is no need to stand on ceremony, or our subject will draw buzzards instead of a bear, get your blank laminated, and let's go.

1. Your most valuable pencil line is the centerline. Because of the spring of the ribs and independent suspension of the hind legs, you'll notice the backbone angles sharply uphill to the hips, gradually sloping down toward the shoulder. Begin to form this critical ridge by cutting from the highest point of the hip toward the backbone, from hip to rump first, top and bottom. Next, there's a sagging hollow in the flank just ahead of the hip that goes all the way to the belly. It is only a slight depression on the underside.

The bulge of the ribs forms the highest point of the body; it's all downhill from there! The little hollow at the back edge of the shoulder shows on the bottom as well as the top. First, slope the stepped edge of the blank down to merge with the lower level, then slope the front of the shoulders a little more.

Because the antlers prop up the head, the neck is a little twisted. Its mane should hit the ground in front. The elk's angular head is tilted so that the jaw slopes downward. The sag of the underside ear is important and can be done in a sketchy way with your larger tools, as is also the case with the other ear, flopped against the neck.

2. We are dealing with a fresh kill here. So we need to make those legs look really collapsed. When flopped on his side like this, the high point on the legs is their attachment to the body. Starting there, visualize carefully the slope you need to give the legs, mainly from the body to the next joint, hock or knee. The lower parts of the legs are more nearly parallel to the ground.

AutoMach carvers can commence carving from the body down the legs; Foredom users will have a better time of it if they work from either end. First, remove the stepped layer edges of the blank into a slope. Break the slope's momentum in the middle by changing the angle at the lower leg.

3. Your larger tools won't allow much differentiation in the levels of the legs on the underside. Switch to a small gouge, or a dovetail burr if you've got one. Because the legs underneath are mashed into the ground, they only taper where there's more muscle concentrated in their upper parts.

4. Now, it is not essential to carve the narrow gap between the pairs of legs since the finished piece will be so low on the base that this opening will barely be visible. However, you may be surprised by how many people are going to look and marvel that you were so thorough. This opening can be simplified. Rather than cutting successively deeper trenches from front and rear until you succeed in tunneling through somewhere in the middle, select a drill with a diameter about equal to the width of the slot. It will be a bigger drill for

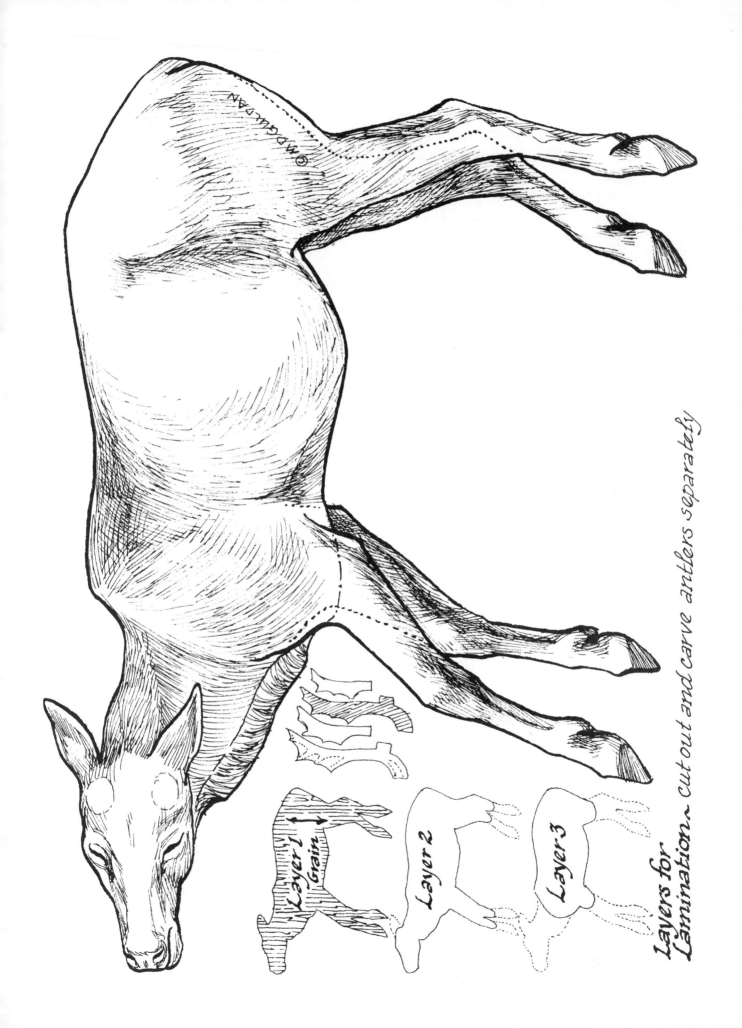

MAGWMAN

Layer 1
Grain

Layer 2

Layer 3

Layers for
Lamination... Cut out and carve antlers separately

a wider space in back, a smaller one in front. Steadily holding your piece up on end, as it is easier to drill down accurately than it is to drill across, drill at one end of the hind leg gap until the drill emerges out the other side. Then drill a second hole at the other end.

Brace him on a pad of folded towels with his legs sticking up. Poke the point of your detail knife into the top hole, blade edge headed toward the bottom hole. By slicing firmly, cut your way to the bottom hole. Remove the knife and make a second slice parallel to the first, splitting out the chip between. Wow, what a nifty little hole! It's a simple matter, then, to cut the ends in a v-shape and add the rounded contour to the upper leg, blending the hole's edges into the leg muscles. Now repeat the procedure, slicing from the joint toward the body to clear the gap between the forelegs.

5. Let's start texturing the surface, doing some final modeling at the same time. (While you may have done the ambling elk all buttery fat with subtle modeling using abrasives, and you reason that an otherwise fit animal who drowned trying to cross a rain swollen river will not yet have lost his body fat—wait a minute.) The finish is descriptive; if your Indian just shot this elk, yes, indeed do him all fat and slick with abrasives. If the elk drowned and is being appropriated by a bear, a more rugged, sketchy surface done with your shallow gouge is best, so that the dead animal will look slightly bedraggled.

In either event, never mind the muscle you put on that other animal; this one needs to sag. Between the point of his hip and the rear of his pelvis, below his tail, he sags. Collapse the hams of his legs together. Genital detail barely shows, and his tail, stumpy as it is, droops. The hip on the bottom squashes a little bulge of meat.

The hollow in the flank should be especially pronounced where the hide drops over the back edge of the rib cage. The back edge of the shoulder blade was buried in a bulge of muscle; now the transition is a gradual curve over relaxed tissue. The tension is instead in the twisted neck. Now you can define the ears and make the mane really drop.

6. Switch to your knife to finish the shapes of the ears and work on the angular planes of the face. Displacing the lower jaw because of the weight of the antlers and head is a good little touch of authenticity.

7. Attend to the soles of the hooves, too, in the interest of accuracy. Since this piece does not have to be fastened to the base by pegs in the soles of his feet, take your burning pen and, starting at the toe of each hoof, cut that cleft between the cleats clear through, from the toes all the way to the coronet, the band where the hair stops and the nail sprouts. Use the tip of your detailing knife to trim a tiny sliver from between the cleats, noting that it widens just a little in the center and narrows at top and bottom. Do this from the front and bottom of each hoof.

Next round the heelbulbs, I like to do this with back-to-back gouge strokes, a procedure that would be less chancy if this pair of curves were outlined with the burning pen and trimmed round with the detailing knife. Use the burning pen to stop cut the dewclaws. Since the elk won't have to stand, the dewclaws can be undercut from underneath so they

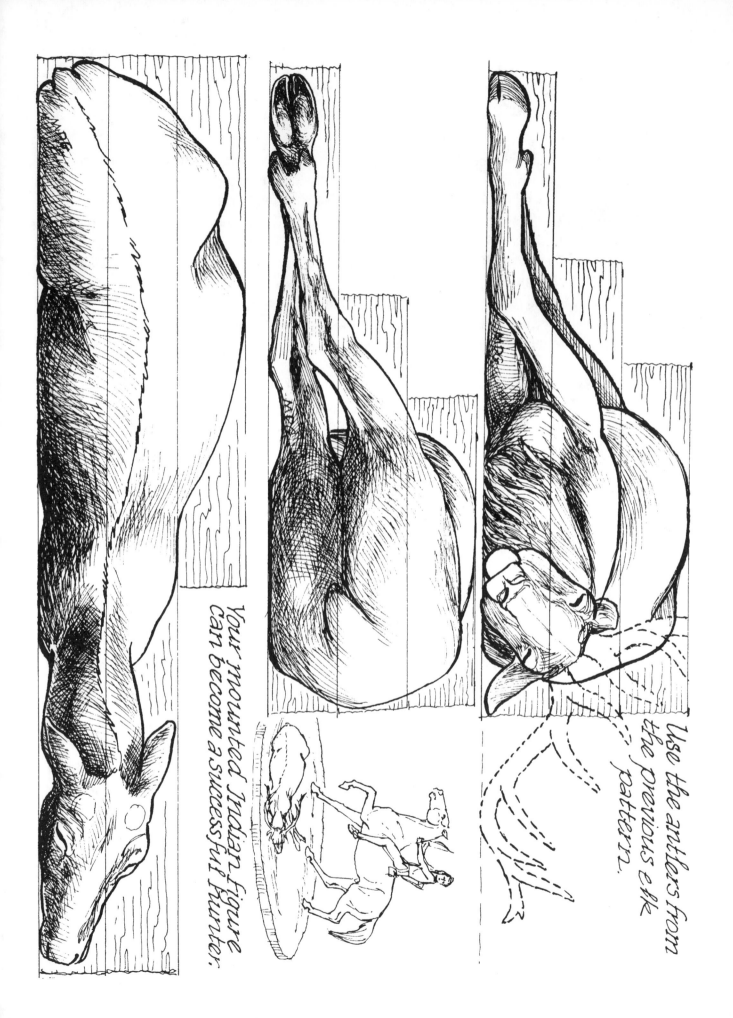

Your mounted Indian figure
can become a successful hunter.

Use the antlers from
the previous elk
pattern.

stick out, a little like the vestigial first and fourth toes left over from prehistoric times, as they actually are.

Use your tiny sphere cutter to hollow the little depression between the heels and dew-claws. The back of the hoof's sole is rounded and rubbery, but between the sides of the v-shaped toes, there is a slight depression to give this animal great traction, which you can hollow the least little bit with that sphere cutter. (Well, not such a good grip after all...)

8. Anyway, somebody hungry stands to profit here! You'll take your burning pen and cut coarse hair in matted clumps along the mane. Make the collapsed nostril slots and the slits between the eyelids.

Well, for a dead elk, he's looking pretty good now. I hope you are doing as well, because you'll need to carve a rack of antlers for this beast. Use the pattern from the live elk and the procedure employed on the caribou. These are awfully fragile, fiddly things, and it seems like you carved the whole animal in less time than it takes to do one antler....

Carve and fit this splendid rack, but wait until after the base has been prepared and textured to glue them permanently in place. Put down a protective layer of plastic, like a shopping bag, and glue the downside antler in place so it touches the ground. Monitor the conduct of the top antler, which may sneak in a little rotation unless you strap masking tape over its insertion site and the butt of the antler.

9. Paint or stain can be effective here. The stain you might make up for yourself. Burnt umber in a turpentine solvent, penetrating oil finish, like Watco Danish Oil, is quite handsome. If you decide to do this project in technicolor, remember that the quality of his coat color is going to be as descriptive as its texture. For the live elk or the one just killed by the Indian, seal the wood first. The color you float on top of this will be a little translucent and have a livelier look. For the grizzly's dead elk, sink the pigment directly into the surface with no primer.

The body hairs are several shades lighter than the extremities; test your mixture on a scrap, starting with a little burnt umber and a good bit of white. If it looks pinkish on your wood, mix in a little raw umber. You are looking for a light sandy brown, which needs to be applied from shoulder to rump. Add more white to this mix for the light rump patch shown on the rear view of the ambling elk. Put a little of this inside the ears and around the eyes, as well as on the tips of the antler tines.

When this has dried, your elk's head, neck, chest, belly, and legs need to be dark brown; using straight burnt umber should do it. If your brand of paint seems more inclined toward rust than brown, settle it down with some raw umber and a very small dab of black. The antlers get a thinned coat of this color washed on, getting lighter and lighter toward the polished tips of the tines.

Mix burnt umber and black until the color is neither one or the other. Use this for the hooves, dewclaws, nose, and eyes. Add a little clear, glossy glaze (compatible with your paint) to the eyes and nose to make them look moist. Now it's time to mount the hunter.

Mounted Indian

SOONER or later, one of your scenes is going to need a mounted figure, and while this is a specific one, Hinmatowyalahtqit (Thunder Coming Up Over the Land), of the Nez Perce, anglicized to Chief Joseph, this is the way one rides without stirrups. The splendid frieze of horsemen carved on the Parthenon, a Greek temple built in Athens in the 5th century B.C., are sitting on their mounts exactly like this, just as you may have done yourself when riding a young horse bareback. Your adductor and gracilis muscles strapped your pelvis to your thigh and helped you fit to the horse's back like a forked stick, as you found a little purchase in the barely perceptible hollow back of the mount's shoulder blades. You sat back with your knees rather far forward, giving you a little leverage against being catapulted over the horse's head in a sudden stop. Your lower legs and feet hung relatively relaxed until you needed to tighten your calves and pinch your mount's ribs, causing him to tense his muscles and run. If he didn't, a swift kick amidships usually reinforced that command.

You can turn this figure into any bareback rider of any era. Let's talk about Chief Joseph (1840–1904) who, had he lived in another time and place, would have been widely honored for his abilities as statesman, soldier, and diplomat. The Nez Perce lived in the Wallowa Valley in Oregon. Unlike other tribes, they bred their horses for quality, not just quantity, and are credited with developing a durable saddle horse often distinguished by its spotted coat—sometimes solid white with an all-over spotted pattern, or more interesting yet, a roan body with a spotted white rump. The horses had sparse manes and tails, an acquired taste to many of us, but a practical aspect to the Indians. Short hair didn't collect burrs or cause maintenance problems! The horses had striped hooves, and the sclera of their eyes showed. Blanket patterned horses with the spotted white rumps, usually were bald-faced, or had white faces, with an odd sprinkling of dark hairs like an eyebrow arched over each eye. If the hair nearest the eye was dark, the eyes were brown; if the hair nearby was white, however, the eye was blue. Because the white markings tended to be irregular, a horse might have one blue eye and the other brown! In an effort to halt the Indian's mobility, the horses were confiscated and most were destroyed by the government. A few, however, wound up in the hands of the settlers, and became the foundation for the Appaloosa breed, which today looks like a spotted quarterhorse.

If you turn this figure into one of the Plains Indians, a favored color pattern was a white horse spotted in rusty red, with one of the red patches occurring over the crown of the head and ears, sort of like a war bonnet. The horses seemed to have been, like four-leafed clovers, a sort of lucky charm. Their name, roughly translated, meant "Medicine Hat." They, too, sometimes had glass or blue eyes, or one blue and one brown, which does give a horse a kind of crazed look, intimidating to an enemy Indian.

Mounted Indian

Take a minute to look over the details. While hunters often went out belted into a breechclout and wearing moccasins, there were elaborate costumes to be worn on occasions of state. Many photographs of Chief Joseph wearing these articles of clothing still exist. Here, the fringed buckskin shirt decorated with plaques of porcupine quilling has been combined with a pair of baggy dark pants trimmed with light braid, actually worn by another Nez Perce, Looking Glass, in an 1870 photo, from which we've taken his bow and arrow as well.

Decide on how you would like to have your figure dressed so that you can make a pattern with any necessary inclusions for costume addition. You will also need to add an appropriate tail for the horse of your choice. Medicine Hats had a regular full tail, reaching below their hocks; Appaloosas had a sparse one, not as long as their hocks. Add a mane if you like.

1. The blank itself is not a complicated one; as with Mr. John, we will leave the arms off until the figure has been carved. When your blank has been constructed and is ready to use, pencil on the horse's dorsal view and the fronts and backs of his legs. Draw the locations of Chief Joseph's legs on the sides of the blank. Mark the shape of his turned head as seen from above on the top of the blank. Draw a line straight down the side of the blank indicating where his nose is to be centered. On the dorsal-view diagram, check Chief Joseph's shoulders, where you will find two dots sneaked in to help you locate that bone nearest the surface at the top of your arm.

2. The technique that's going to be exciting to learn is how to give this figure a believable, lively pose, so that you're not stranded doing a face-forward pose. Research this shoulder point on your own arm as you read along. Feel around up there, and just about buried in softer muscle is the top of your humerus, the big arm bone. Try leaning one elbow on the table as you prop your chin in your hand, thinking this over. Put the other hand on your hip. Without having to go out and catch and mount your horse, you've twisted your body around at your chest just like Chief Joseph. The curve across the front corresponds to a curve across your back, forming an elongated oval, with your arms at the narrow ends. This oval does not change configuration just because it was pivoted.

Fix this idea in mind. Take your ruler and bridge the diagram's dots, memorize that tilt! Mark those dots on your blank; we're going to make them work for you!

Now, as in the Indianapolis 500 car race.... "Gentlemen, start your engines!"

3. Using your largest tools, the AutoMach gouge or your ball-nosed carbide burr, start at the horse's hips, first knocking off the square corners between the points of the hips and the dock of the tail, then gently round over the top of the platform. Check the rear view for the leading edges of the hind legs; the stifle, knee-type joint on the right sticks out a tad farther, ahead of the striding leg. The stifle is located where the horse's leg leaves his barrel. On both sides, these project farther than the points of the hips, so cut this angle. From the leading edges of the hind legs, as is apparent in the dorsal view, the sides of the

Layers for lamination
Check text; add appropriate
tail (and mane) to pattern

Cut out arms

Grain
Layer 1

Layer 2

Layer 3

Layer 4

actual size for ¾ inch thick lumber

Frederic Remington painting of an Indian scout, also appears in drawings by Indians

from George Catlin, c. 1830's

from Charles M. Russell paintings

from 1871 photograph of Looking Glass, Nez Percé

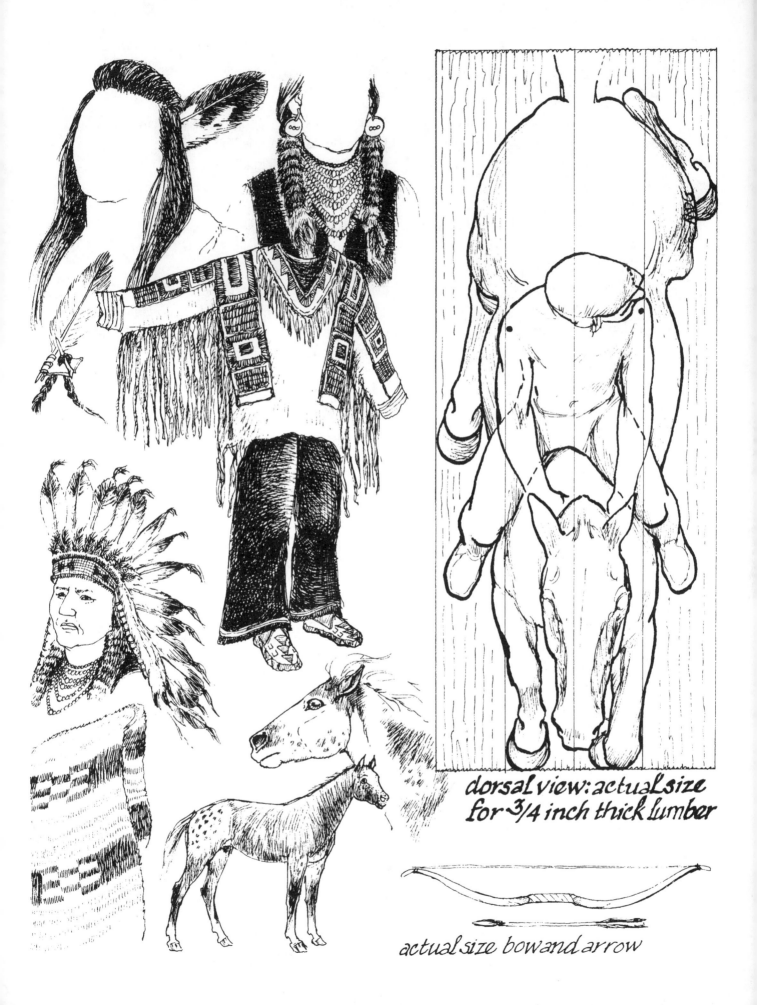

dorsal view: actual size
for 3/4 inch thick lumber

actual size bow and arrow

rump curve toward each other in back.

There's quite of lot of waste on the outsides of the horse's thighs, as you can see by your outline. For better access, why not cut to that outside profile line all the way to the bottom of the hoof. Then you can round off the horse's rump in all directions.

Next, if you Foredom users have a pretty hefty dovetail, it can be a real asset for the next process.

Your most grave temptation here, will be that you get so fascinated with cutting around the Indian's legs that you plow a trench right into his horse. Rein in your enthusiasm! Check the dorsal views of your mule and horses. Without anyone in the way on their backs, you can see how egg-shaped their rib cages are, narrow end foremost.

Take off! There's a lot of waste around the horse's ribs; they need to be smaller than his haunches. There's a dotted line on the rear-view diagram outlining their largest point. The dotted Indian leg lines on the front suggest how the ribs narrow. They are more peaked right behind the shoulders and fuller at the bottom (so you won't worry about where this charger puts his lungs.)

Don't leave extra wood for the trailing end of the breechclout. Knock off the blank's square corners first, rounding more and more until the swell no longer bulges fatter than the haunches. Right behind the Indian's seat, the backbone forms a little ridge which broadens as it meets the hips. The ribs are quite rounded along the bottom edge, gradually narrowing back of the elbows of the horse's forelegs.

Leave the Indian's legs just squared platforms until we get the horse's front end roughed out. Since the head and neck, from the front, are basically flattened shapes with parallel sides, let's start up there so that we can get the flow of this pose. You've got room, if you'd like, to turn the horse's head more to the right or left. Just draw an oval muzzle on the front of the blank, bisected by a line that goes right up the middle of the horse's face. Cross that line at a right angle at eye level, the widest point of the horse's skull. Cut off the sides of the blank from eye to muzzle, then from eye to neck, then down the sides of the neck, gradually widening at the shoulder.

The front edges to the shoulders form little shelves shaped like inverted right angles. This is noticeable from the sides; from the front, the widest part of the shoulders is the muscle bulge right above the forearm.

Go on and cut the outside profile of the forelegs; you have enough experience in being careful not to mash on them and break them. If they break on their own, because wood does have those unaccountable weak places, mend them with a hardwood dowel peg or brass rod for stability and go on about your carving. Those things will happen.

4. Before you go about clearing between the horse's legs, let's rough out the rider. By now you will have handled this piece enough so that the prospects are not so daunting. During all of his adult life, it would seem, Chief Joseph wore the hair on his crown cropped in an upstanding roach. So round off the top of the head only a little, from front to back,

Mounted Indian

and leave room for this. Your pencil line the length of his nose is the next target, as it shows the direction of his face. Cut from the corners of his (eventual) cheeks to make the nose stick up like the leading edge of a very broad wedge. The back of his head is rounded, even with his hair dangling. And there's a good bit of waste there, so start cutting! Check constantly, from the back view especially, to get the correct distance between the face and back of the head.

5. Now, find those shoulder dots; cut across his back, using those dots to anchor a broad curve that is closer to the front on one side. There's a corresponding curve, though less of one, to be cut across the front.

From there, cut down either side of the back, first to your profile line, leaving the body square. Draw a reminder oval on the flat side of each shoulder where arms will later attach. Then go on and round the corners of the body, right down to his seat on the horse.

Oh terror, now we work on his legs! Change to smaller tools if you need. There's quite a large reserve of waste, so you've got a ways to go. Locate the Indian's knee. Our thigh bones tend to be rather straight, so cut from the knee to the thigh's point of attachment at the hip. It may take a while to get there.

From the hip, round the front of the trunk, merging with the chest curve cut earlier.

Then take on the lower legs and feet. Make a slight curve for the fullness of the calf and turn the feet out just the least little bit.

6. Since the horse's legs are our biggest fragile projections, let's just leave them for the time being, and take on the completion of shaping in the less vulnerable areas, getting a finished surface as we do so. If your detail knife has a curved sabre clip blade, so much the better. Brace your carving against that folded and bundled up towel in the back of your bench hook and, two-handing your knife, start on your horse's hips, shaving them into shape with many small, probably shallow, scoops. After the hips and rump, take on the back of the barrel and the crevice where the Indian's legs lie. Pencil in that leg outline again, but be very cautious as you stop cut along it not to plunge your knife tip too deep, scarring the horse.

First, obtain the sharp outline of the backs of the legs meeting the barrel at a right angle. Then, when the barrel's been authentically rounded (this time leaving room for the trailing breechclout), begin to undercut the legs.

This need not be deep, but it will certainly look exciting! Start your cut from the shape of the barrel, which your knife will follow tractably anyway, then go back and round the whole leg, following through on that cut until it meets the barrel undercut, nipping out a wedge-shaped sliver.

At the ankles, the narrow Achille's tendon causes a widening gap between the feet and the horse's body.

7. If this was hard on your nerves, you might do your next shaping up the Indian's back. But if you are fired up with excitement over seeing this leg start to emerge, go on to do the front of the leg since you are so focused on the shapes involved.

Warm up by smoothing the horse's shoulders ahead of that leg. Their sides have a slight curve; they are wider at the front than in back and have a peak at the top where the roots of the mane terminate.

Now, pencil in the exact outline of the front of each leg. Give this guy a real knee! Reach down and feel your own kneecap. It's a hard little bone protecting the hinged joint underneath, causing a pretty sharp-angled bend at the front of the leg. If you don't want your horseman to look all noodley, you'll see that he has knees.

Carve them first. Make the little knee cap point straight ahead. Don't undercut too much there, as the bones of the leg fit pretty tightly into a pocket of equine shoulder muscles there. The roundness of the fronts of the thighs can be undercut right to the edge of Chief Joseph's breechclout.

The lower legs have a more open angle as they meet the horse, caused by the edge of bone you'll feel down the front of your own leg. Trim his moccasins into shape, remembering that their soles as well are foot-shaped.

8. In his lap, the trailing edge of the breechclout probably swung underneath as he vaulted onto the horse, and is being sat on. Your consideration is that, like his shoulders, his hips, too, are tilted; one side forward the other back. Use a little, small sphere burr on the belt line to cut a slight curve across the belly with one end nearer the horse's neck; the other end is pushed back. From that point, the crotch is a slightly hollowed v shape, so the legs can be seen pointing forward.

Refine your work as you smooth and detail the trunk.

9. Carving character into a face as small as this means that the detailing is going to be simplified and basic. Because the nose is the most projecting central feature, begin there by first cutting the profile into that ridge reserved for it. This will be a series of notches, first top and bottom of nose, then hairline and chin.

Do the forehead first, sloping back from brows toward hairline; you'll be encouraged by your competence.

Next, establish the shape of the chin and the very firm jaw.

Use your tiny sphere cutter on either side of the bridge of the nose to help start the hollow for eyesockets. A little notch with your detailing knife can finish it. Round the cheeks, but do not be overly generous. The back edges of the cheeks are not level with their fronts, and then they bend back toward the ears.

If this piece is to be painted or stained, your burning pen with a tight, round little tip can surely do this tiny detailing well. Use it to draw in the eye openings; doing them as narrowed slots makes them suitably distant and brooding. The burning pen will also do the flare of the nostrils and the separation between the lips. Use the tiny sphere cutter on the hollow beneath the lower lip and at the corners of the mouth.

Shape the basic hair masses, using your burning pen to texture them, and detail the ears. Hollow below the earlobe, between the braids and around the loose hair with the tiny sphere.

Go ahead and define the belt and the folds and edges of the breechclout; they aren't particularly fragile, and you'll have them done.

10. Now that Chief Joseph has turned into a person for you, you might want to take a break and read up on him. He gets only cursory notice in the history of the settlers' westward expansion overall, but check for a biography in the juvenile section of your public library. In an effort to educate, several excellent biographies and biographical sketches have been written about him, one illustrated with the Edward Curtis photos that make his haunted eyes almost too memorable. The events are simply told; they are simply tragic.

Public television stations in your area probably subscribe to a series of book reviews for children called *Reading Rainbow.* Many stations will arrange to lend the half-hour programs. They are masterfully produced. Check on the one featuring Paul Goble's book, *The Gift of the Sacred Dog,* which includes a wonderful segment on young Indians riding bareback across the prairies, as well as a segment on the Crow Fair, a huge pow-wow.

11. Now, go to work on the horse's face, doing all of the detailing except hollowing the horses nostrils. If you chose to bridle the horse with a thong, you can either carve the headstall, or make it out of glue-soaked string.

12. At this point, if you are accustomed to dealing with more fragile carvings, proceed with roughing out the insides of the legs and go on and finish them, following the same procedures used in doing the mule.

If you are a little uneasy about working around the legs, do Chief Joseph's arms next. As with Mr. John, carve the hands and lower arms first to a just above the elbow. If your figure is to be turned into a hunter, change the dotted opened hand to a closed one.

There is a correctly scaled bow pattern, taken from a bow in the Looking Glass portrait. To keep this from being too fragile consider making it from wire coated with successive layers of epoxy until the center is built up, making the ends look tapered.

Your burning pen can certainly help you separate fingers. If Chief Joseph is to hold anything, drill a hole of that size through his closed first from top to bottom, but don't risk breaking this hand by threading the object through. When his arms are on and finished, cut the object where his hand will be holding it, inserting the bow or thong rein in from both the top and bottom of the fist.

While it's on your mind, the bow can be strung when its glue has dried. Cut yourself a piece of heavy sewing thread as long as the bow, with some extra for handholds for yourself on each end. Drag the bowstring length through glue (epoxy will work quickly). Wrap the thread quickly several turns around the bottom of the bow, while the glue is still quite gummy. Then pull the thread up and wrap it several turns around the bow's top.

The thread usually is too sticky to untwist itself, but should it show any inclination, just hold its ends to prevent this for a few minutes until the epoxy begins to cure. When that is done, snip off the extra thread and the bow's strung!

Now, after that diverging thought, check the procedure used to put the arms on Mr. John. This will work just as well for Chief Joseph.

When Chief Joseph has his arms on, and the horse's legs and hooves have been completed, in whichever order, the last thing to be done is the horse's tail. We've saved it for last because it would have broken off so easily if accidentally leaned on earlier.

Even now, brace it from the other side against the edge of your workbench, taking care not to crush a leg as you use a large burr or coarse abrasives to round over the top of the tail, tapering it toward the bottom and tip. Use finer abrasives to sand it into shape, letting the abrasives form little ripples and hollows that will give your burning pen an interesting surface on which to work.

By now, you are so near the finish you can just see the way you're going to display this figure. You're excited, and it's just as well. But don't get so excited that you lose sight of the last few details. These hair strokes on the tail can not be even. They need to be short, clustered versions of that bear fur pattern, without the curves in the strokes. Burn them in overlapping layers, not single unbroken lines from top to bottom. Speaking of that bottom edge, clean your blade-shaped pen tip and burn upward in hair direction slicing a deep notch. Oh, wow, it's looking really hairy!

Not too many of those now, it will spoil the effect. Instead, do a few of those double-stroke hair clumps, (such as described in the bear hair) making a little sliver come loose. If your tail is thin enough to allow, cut a few of those all the way through to make little button-hole shaped openings in the clumped tail hair. Don't start a fire!

While the horse's tail and your pen cool down, very gently hollow the horse's nostrils with your tiny sphere cutter.

There! Look what you've done!

It seems like a trifling intrusion to mention stain or paint here, but since you've already decided what you want to do, this is only a technical point. Judging by the photographs of him, Chief Joseph's skin tone was very dark. It would seem, judging by tones of known objects in these antique black and white photos, that a mixture of a little burnt sienna into burnt umber will give you the dark reddish-brown you need. Test it on a scrap first; if it looks too rusty, try tempering it with a little raw umber. If it is too much like ash brown, try a tiny amount of red. This color would be very appropriate for a stain for the entire carving, as well as for just skin, should you choose to realistically paint in detail.

What a splendid figure! Be especially sure to sign and date this one!

REVERSE!

Obverse!

Now that I've told you what I know, it's your turn! Add what you've learned and pass it on, giving the next person the boost.

We've got a vital commission, you and I. We've got to give people back their sense of wonder.

"How'd you do that?" They say when they see your display.

more like _I don't see how you did that! ... Neither do I.

They're used to the incredible electronic wizardry that makes phenomenal illusions take shape on movie screens, in theme parks all over the place. They already know that sophisticated computer programming makes the impossible_visible, on that flickering screen. It's all an illusion.

And then, here you are! Unplugged. No floppy disc, or beeping and boinging. No keyboard...if you had a mouse, you'd zap that sucker with D·Con! (They get in your toolbox and... rust your tools, y'know.) Anybody who ever toted firewood, or picked up after a storm knows about wood_ hard, heavy, splintery_intractible!

Yet, you took that stuff_and you made this stuff! It's no illusion, it's a whole little world you can walk all the way around, and look at from every angle... Hey, is this from a kit? I betcha it's plastic....How'd you do that? In few jobs today does a craftsman see an entire project from concept to completion. So, how'd you do that? (You look so_ordinary. I'll bet it's in your wood. It's special...)

Well, didn't we fool them?! We gave the viewers something wholesome to marvel at. They don't know_we turn into wizards when we walk into our workshops! M.D.G.

Index